A SOCIAL HISTORY OF
THE EARLY
CHURCH

Simon M. Jones

Published by
Lion Hudson Limited
Wilkinson House, Jordan Hill Business Park
Banbury Road, Oxford OX2 8DR, England
www.lionhudson.com

ISBN 978 1 9125 5218 4
e-ISBN 978 1 9125 5219 1

First hardback edition 2011

Acknowledgments
Scripture quotations are the author's own translations.

p. 10 map: Richard Watts of Total Media Services

p. 30 illustration: DEA PICTURE LIBRARY/De Agostini/Getty Images

Cover image: London, the tiled mosaic of Old Testament scenes with the patriarchs Melchizedek, Moses and Abraham, in All Saints Church, by Matthew Digby Wyatt (1820–1877) © sedmak / istockphoto.com

A catalogue record for this book is available from the British Library

Printed and bound in the United Kingdom

CONTENTS

ACKNOWLEDGMENTS

No book is a solo enterprise – though sometimes, late at night when you feel you are the only person awake in the house, or early in the morning when you are bleary-eyed with a day of writing lying ahead of you, it feels like it.

This book is the product of learning at the feet of great scholars and story-tellers who have shared their learning both personally and in countless books and journal articles devoured over the years.

I am not an expert in ancient history or New Testament studies. I am a writer and teacher of New Testament studies with a masters in the social, economic and physical location of the earliest Christian communities. I hope some of what I have uncovered and the enthusiasm that buoyed me on my journey of discovery comes across in what follows.

It just remains for me to thank the one person I couldn't have done this without: Linda, my wife of thirty-seven years, who has unstintingly and lovingly supported me through this project, as she has through all the previous ones. This one's for you.

Simon M. Jones

BEGIN HERE . . .

This book is not an exhaustive treatment of the subject – not a compendium of everything there is to know about the Roman empire and the place of the earliest Christian groups within it.

But it is designed to fill in some of the blanks and whet your appetite to find out more. There is a whole smörgåsbord of resources at the back of this book that will take you further into an amazing world.

In some ways this is an old-fashioned book in that it's designed to be read consecutively, from chapter 1 to chapter 8. You can dip in and out using the contents page, and you should be able to find the fact or insight that you are looking for. But reading the whole thing will give you a good overview, a flavour of the daily lives of those ordinary men and women who were the first to join the Christian church in the cities around the Roman world from the mid-30s to the mid-60s AD.

The evidence about the Christian communities we look at in this book comes almost exclusively from a collection of letters written by a leader of the Christian movement, a tent-maker from Tarsus in modern-day Turkey, a fiery Jewish intellectual who had been an opponent of the Christians in the early days but who changed his mind following an encounter on the Damascus road that he claimed was with the risen Jesus. His name was Paul.

We also include evidence from other parts of the New Testament, especially the Acts of the Apostles, a history of the early Christian movement written by a close associate of Paul's called Luke.

A fresh page

The church was born in the years near the beginning of the imperial age. Octavian had become Augustus Caesar, *princeps* (or emperor) of Rome, in 27 BC. It was a time of hope and expectation, of economic growth and

Archaeology, Artefacts, and Books

How do we know about the past? This apparently simple question has spawned a library filled with books on the methods of historians and how scholars sift and weigh the evidence to create a narrative of bygone ages.

There are two types of evidence available to people who study the ancient world, the world of the early church. These are often called "physical" and "literary".

Physical remains refer to anything that can be dated to a particular period – buildings, statues, household goods, and documents. The Roman world comes to life in such places as Pompeii and Ostia in Italy, Ephesus and Aphrodisias in Turkey, Athens and Corinth in Greece, Caesarea Maritima and Jerusalem in Israel/Palestine.

Archaeologists are able to piece together the evidence yielded by such sites to create stories of the everyday lives of the people who occupied these sites when they were living communities. It is not a precise science, however. The archaeological record is patchy, and teams of scholars have to work with what they can handle and combine it with what they already know of the period they are studying in order to generate theories which are then tested against subsequent research.

Literary evidence refers to the contents of books and papers, inscriptions on walls, and other written records. Among the literary remains that we have from the world of the early Christians are the writings that comprise the New Testament, twenty-seven books and letters that were written over a fifty-year period from the late 40s AD. But we also have the writings of Roman historians and philosophers, those of Jewish thinkers (such as Philo and Josephus), and collections of commercial records and personal correspondence that are turned up from time to time by archaeologists.

One such collection is a wealth of papyrus documents unearthed in the Egyptian city of Oxyrhynchus that has thrown light on the concerns of ordinary householders and government officials, many from the time of the Roman empire.

There are two problems with literary evidence. The first is that we invariably only have copies of documents, not the originals. This is because the materials that books and scrolls are written on do not last. So copies have to be made to preserve the ideas. It means that we can never be absolutely certain when a particular document was first written. We have to piece together the likely date from physical evidence and what we know about the life and circumstances of the author. The major exception to this are the many papyri that are original documents of all kinds, including personal letters, contracts, bills of lading and so on.

The second is that writers have a particular view of things, seeing the world their way, which is not always the way other people see it. So when Roman writers tell us about the lives of the poor, it is difficult to know how objective they are being since they were invariably members of the privileged elite.

In this book, we make the best use we can of the evidence at our disposal, both physical and literary, to create a narrative of the world of the early church.

grinding poverty, of expansion and consolidation of the most spectacular empire the world had ever seen.

Jesus of Nazareth had been born in the reign of Augustus, probably around 6 BC, and had begun his ministry under the emperor Tiberius. The church began emerging in the mid-30s in the cities at the eastern end of the empire – Jerusalem, Caesarea, Antioch, and Damascus. By the AD 40s it had reached Rome, Athens, the cities of Galatia (the central part of modern-day Turkey), Thessalonica, and Philippi. In the 50s it reached Corinth, Ephesus, and the Mediterranean islands.

The church found a small foothold in the back streets of these bustling cities. This is a description of the soil in which it took root and the lives lived by the earliest urban followers of Jesus.

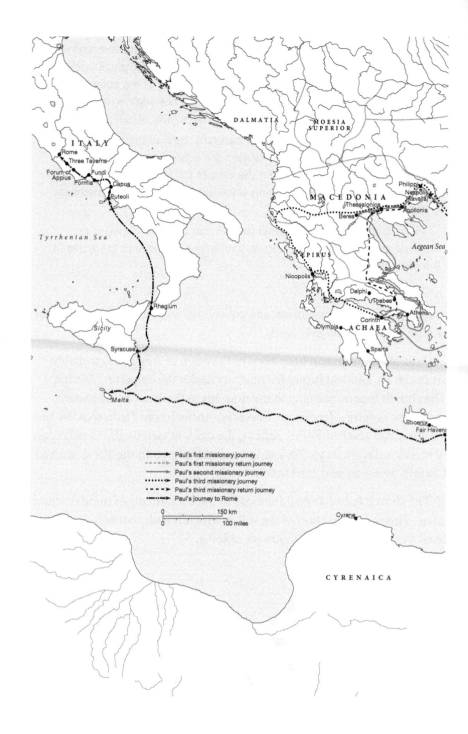

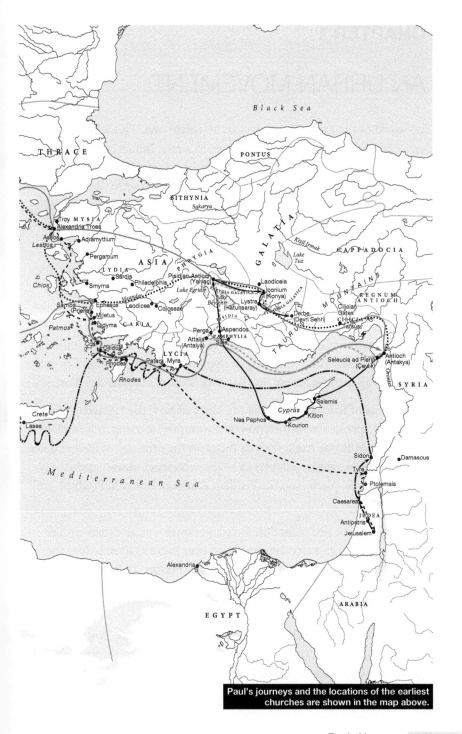

Paul's journeys and the locations of the earliest churches are shown in the map above.

CHAPTER 1

AN URBAN MOVEMENT

The world of the early Christians was an urban one. This is not to say that everyone in the Roman world lived in a city. In fact only about a fifth of the empire's population lived in urban areas. Nor were there necessarily no followers of Jesus who lived on farms or in tiny villages: there probably were. But we only really know about the progress of the first Christians in cities.

Apart from the letter of James, which was written to scattered communities in rural Galilee and Judea, everything we know about the lives of the early Christians comes from an urban context. So we read of Philemon living in Colossae, Timothy in Ephesus, and Phoebe in the port city of Cenchrea; we have two of Paul's four letters to the Roman city of Corinth in Greece and another to the Roman colony of Philippi. Even Peter's letters and John's Apocalypse are written to small Christian groups living in cities across Roman Asia Minor (modern-day Turkey).

The Acts of the Apostles tells the story of how the Christian movement spread across the cities of the empire, starting in Jerusalem and ending in Rome itself, with its focus on the ministry of Paul and his colleagues (especially in chapters 13–28), who work almost exclusively in Roman cities, places such as Pisidian Antioch, Corinth, Philippi, and Thessalonica.

The reason for this is that the Roman empire was an urban empire. Rome was the largest city the world had ever known. Even before the birth of Jesus, its population was nudging a million. There would only be another city as big when London topped the million mark in the late eighteenth century.

Rome was not the only substantial city in the empire. Antioch, Alexandria, Athens, Corinth, Ephesus, Pergamum, and Sardis were all significant conurbations, though considerably smaller than the capital, with populations of between 50,000 and 200,000.

Cities were the places where power lay. Rome, of course, was the centre of the world as far as Romans (who called the shots across most of the known world at the time) were concerned! It was the seat of power (where the emperor lived and the senate met), a place of immense wealth, the centre of a spider's web of imperial trade that spread east and west across most of the known world, even beyond the borders of the empire itself to India and China.

It was also teeming with the urban poor who lived in makeshift homes in overcrowded ghettos. Indeed, population density in Rome and other ancient cities was higher than it is in most modern cities. Rome was more like Mumbai than Paris. Its population was crammed into a small space, making its streets narrow and crowded and its buildings overflow with people. The density of population was of the order of 730 people per hectare compared with just 452 for Mumbai. And all ancient cities were similar.

Films depicting the lives of emperors and the Roman elite – such as *Ben Hur* and *Gladiator* – give the impression that life in the empire's cities was pretty comfortable, if not opulent. Even slaves appear to have eaten and dressed well! But for most urban dwellers in the first century, life was hard, with daylight hours given over to trying to find enough to live on. Living conditions were rudimentary, with little in the way of home comforts or basic sanitation.

Earning a crust

Historians are divided on what economic life was like in the first Christian century. Some argue that the Roman empire was a vast single market, with goods being traded from city to city and ships criss-crossing the Mediterranean, loaded with anything from basic foodstuffs to luxury cloth and exotic spices. In this market, many people got rich but even the poor were able to scrape a living.

Others suggest that economic life was decidedly primitive, that there was really nothing approaching a market economy. Rather, wealth resided in land and was controlled by a few well-established, extremely wealthy families. Such trade as there was, was small-scale and in the hands of humbler people; it was certainly frowned on by members of the ruling elite.

As with a lot of historical debates, the truth probably lies somewhere in the middle. There was not a market economy such as we see in the world today. But there was a lively trade in both raw materials and manufactured products. In particular, Rome was a vast market for grain, oil, and wine, as well as manufactured goods such as pottery and clothes. It also imported vast quantities of building materials in the first century as successive emperors built and rebuilt the city, making it ever more glorious.

This meant that the port of Ostia on the coast, twenty-two kilometres to the west of the capital, developed during the first century into a thriving centre of trade with links to every corner of the far-flung empire.

Most cities – probably including Rome itself – were regarded as the conurbation plus the agricultural land that surrounded it, where much of the food for the city was grown. This means that many city people still worked the land, walking each morning from their urban garrets to farm small plots of land. Most of these were tenant farmers, but a few would have been sons or slaves of the landowners themselves.

However, as cities grew, more and more people earned a living away from agriculture. Historians have identified more than 200 different jobs from Rome's tombstones (see chapter 3). These monuments generally mark the remains of skilled people, often men (and it is largely men) who had started as slaves, been trained in trades, and then either earned or bought their freedom and continued in those trades until their deaths.

But most of Rome's citizens were unskilled wage-labourers, selling their muscle daily to anyone who needed it. These people were referred to as *mercennarii*, which is the root of our word "mercenary", and they would be paid by the day to do a variety of tasks, the most common of which was carrying things around. They might be hired to carry supplies from a rich landowner's house to his tenants working the fields outside the city; or they might be hired to collect goods bought in the market and carry them to the new owner's home.

Of course, a major way such unskilled workers earned a living was by labouring on building sites. Throughout the first century, Rome and many other cities across the empire were transformed by massive municipal building projects. For example, a single construction project undertaken by the emperor Claudius employed 30,000 men for eleven years as diggers. The work was hard and badly paid, but at least it ensured that most of these men and their families could eat.

Chapter 7 will cover in more detail the Roman economy and how rich or poor people were. Here, we will attempt to get an overview of ancient cities, looking especially at Rome, Ostia, and Pompeii in Italy, before glancing across the sea at Corinth, Ephesus, and Antioch at the eastern end of the empire.

As Augustus tightened his grip on power over his long reign, he made major changes to the way the city of Rome looked. He claimed that he had come to a city built of brick and left it a marble marvel. And across the empire, local elites aped what Augustus and his successors did in Rome, to show that they were proud and loyal members of this powerful new empire. In this way, Roman imperial rule was felt in the architecture, culture, and street life of cities across Europe, the Middle East, and North Africa. Visitors to most Roman cities across the empire would have found the layout and architecture familiar; they would have known where to go to find the seat of government, to buy or sell goods, to get a meal, or to have a good night out.

A close-up view

Cities were geographically small, tightly packed, and densely populated, drawing to their gates people of all nationalities seeking to earn a crust or make something of themselves. Most were laid out on a grid system, with straight main roads intersecting each other frequently. But city streets were narrow. In Rome there was a law that required streets to be three metres wide – wide enough for several people to pass, but probably not two carts. Even major thoroughfares, such as the Appian Way in Rome, were only four and a half metres across and these were the main supply routes into cities, crowded with carts, animals, and people. Most of the time they would have felt like a stadium at a sporting championship.

Although the Romans are famed for their sanitation, the grim reality was that most drainage consisted of open ditches that ran down the middle of these narrow streets and were filled to overflowing with household waste of all kinds, including the contents of chamber-pots and buckets emptied from second- and third-floor windows first thing in the morning – despite laws prohibiting it. Such was the stench in Rome and other imperial cities that those rich enough retreated in the summer months to villas in the countryside or on the coast to escape the risk of illness as well as the rank odour of the city.

Most households drew their water from public fountains or wells. In Pompeii these were plentiful, with water being brought into the city via an aqueduct and then distributed to a network of fountains situated at the intersections of main routes. It meant that most of the city's inhabitants were never further than 1,000 metres from a source of water for cooking, drinking, and bathing. Not all city-dwellers were as fortunate.

The buildings that lined these narrow streets came in all shapes and sizes. Most were blocks that occupied a whole site between street intersections and are known as *insulae* (see p. 25). Until the second century in Rome, these buildings tended to be only two or three storeys high. The ground floors, facing the street, housed shops and bars, while the rooms behind and upstairs were used as living accommodation of varying size and quality.

These buildings were generally constructed from wood and stucco and hence were very flammable. There were also no chimneys and many families cooked in their one room on a low brazier, venting the smoke to the outside via the doors and windows (if any) of their apartment. Not surprisingly, fires were frequent in the poorer, more overcrowded parts of all cities. Early in his reign, Augustus established guilds of fire-fighters who would patrol the city's streets at night with buckets, ladders, and primitive siphons for spraying water in the hope of stopping fires before they took hold and burned through an entire area. About 7,000 men were recruited as so-called *vigiles*, housed in the various regions of the city.

They did the best they could, but even that many men could not prevent the great fire of Rome in AD 64, which started in the Circus Maximus and raged for nine days, in total severely damaging ten of Rome's fourteen districts, three of which had to be completely demolished. In the rebuilding that followed, streets were widened in the hope of preventing the spread of flames from building to building. Rome was not alone in being the victim of devastating fires. Antioch in the east suffered three accidental conflagrations causing widespread damage over a period of four centuries of Roman rule.

Because of the risk of fire, cooking was a major problem in the *insulae*, so many of their inhabitants got their meals at street corner bars (*popinae*) that sold wine and a variety of simple cooked food. One archaeologist has described these places as a cross between Burger King and a tapas bar. Many people would have sat around these places, eating and chatting. In many ways they were like the bars and cheap cafés of our own cities. But many more would have taken a plate or bowl, bought their meal on the street corner, and returned to their apartment or room to eat with their family.

Taking a tour

Most of the empire's cities were laid out in similar ways: a grid of streets with houses and apartments, areas where municipal buildings and temples clustered around a central square, and others where entertainments of one kind or another were on offer.

Pompeii is in many ways typical. Devastated in August AD 79 by the eruption of Vesuvius that left it buried in pumice and ash for fifteen centuries, it has given archaeologists the fullest guide to urban life at the height of the empire.

The focal point of Pompeii was the civic forum, a large rectangular space at the western end of the town, surrounded by magnificent buildings. One of the reasons for the magnificence of Pompeii at the time it was engulfed by the eruption was that, less than twenty years before, it had been substantially damaged by an earthquake and throughout the 60s and into the 70s the city fathers spent lavishly to rebuild it, hoping that the glories of the new Pompeii would outshine the old.

So, there was a striking basilica and a series of two-storey rectangular buildings, housing the courts and rooms and halls used for banking and business transactions of all kinds, the *curia* (where the city magistrates met), the records office, and the public markets, where meat and fish, olives, wine, and other local produce were sold.

There were also temples. The two important deities were Jupiter and Apollo, who each had a lavish temple complex. The temple to Jupiter was a copy of the one that stood on the Capitoline Hill in Rome. There was also a small but significant temple to the divine Augustus; worship of the emperor was the fastest growing cult in the first century, even in Italy (see chapter 8). The eastern cults were also represented, with temples and shrines to Isis and other exotic foreign deities.

At the other end of the city a 20,000-seater amphitheatre would have played host to gladiatorial combats and other spectacles, while a theatre showed Atellan farces and other dramatic productions to audiences of up to 5,000. There was even a smaller *odeon*, a covered theatre space for smaller, more intimate productions.

Ostia is the other significant Italian city that gives us insight into city life in Roman times. Meaning "mouth", Ostia is located fourteen miles (22 km) from Rome, on the coast where the river Tiber empties into the Mediterranean. Although it is not a natural harbour, it became one of the places where goods destined for Rome were off-loaded to be taken by barge on the last part of the journey up the river. The other was Puteoli on the Bay of Naples, but goods unloaded there had to be transported over land, which was costly and much slower than using the river.

So, Ostia was developed over the years as a port city. At its height, following significant rebuilding and expansion first by Claudius in the AD 40s and then by Trajan at the turn of the second century, it was home to more than 50,000 people and saw thousands of ships come and go each year bringing goods and raw materials bound for the capital.

Although there was no natural harbour at Ostia, Claudius created a huge artificial one measuring some 3,280 feet (1,000 m) in diameter, linked to the city by a network of canals. Here ships could unload in relative safety. Very quickly a substantial working city grew up around this new structure.

The very nature of the place meant that Ostia was a city of *insulae* and warehouses, with very few villa-style houses. The warehouses or *horrea* that lined the harbour and canals were of two basic designs. They were either square constructions built around a central courtyard or rectangular buildings with a double row of rooms placed back to back. They were occupied by merchants, who were responsible for bringing goods and raw materials through the city to Rome.

Many *horrea* had false floors indicating that they were built to house grain, which had to be kept warm and dry so that it did not go off while it was being stored. Vast quantities of grain were required to feed Rome's population and most of it came from the grain fields of Egypt. Because of storms at sea in the winter months, such shipments could only safely be made between May and September, so grain had to be stored in Ostia and shipped up the Tiber at regular intervals to ensure continuity of supply whatever the season.

Other warehouses had stone jars or vats built into the floors for storing wine or olive oil. Many of these containers, called *dolia*, could hold 750 litres and one warehouse has been excavated that had 100 of these, indicating that at any one time it could have housed 75,000 litres of wine or olive oil. This gives some indication of the scale of trade that went through Ostia.

At the centre of the city were the forum and a theatre, various temples, and buildings that were clearly used for administration. One of the most distinctive structures is called the piazza of the corporations, a double colonnaded portico with buildings on three sides containing sixty-one rooms. On the ground in front of each of the buildings are black and white mosaics indicating the trade being handled from each room. Mosaics suggest the presence of shipowners, grain suppliers, wine merchants, and a host of other businesses that brought goods through the port. And more exotic merchants plied their trade in the piazza: importers of wild animals for the spectacles that took place in the amphitheatre and elsewhere in Italy, and slave traders, bringing fresh labour for elite homes and farms from Africa, the Middle East, and Asia.

Night life

While during the day cities were vibrant places full of the bustle of trade and politics, street sellers, and performing philosophers and musicians, at night they changed. The satirist Juvenal exclaimed that to go out to supper without first having made a will was to be guilty of gross carelessness. He was probably exaggerating. But the city streets after sunset became dangerous places to be, as gangs roamed, robbing the hapless who had gone out alone. For this reason, when people of substance did go out for dinner, they were accompanied by slaves carrying torches and clubs. The only people who might come to your aid if you were found alone on the streets by robbers were the patrolling fire-fighters.

But for many city residents, dangerous nights were only one aspect of first-century urban angst. Historians paint a picture of ancient Antioch as a place of misery, danger, fear, despair, and hatred. They point to a city informally zoned into at least eighteen areas, each home to a different ethnic group who defended their turf against outsiders, especially at night, with often lethal force. Riots and disturbances, sparked by the most minor of misunderstandings, were common.

Here the average family lived in squalor in an overcrowded tenement, perhaps crammed into just one room. Most children would lose a parent before reaching adulthood and most parents would bury up to half the live children they produced. Cities were places of isolation where those without any kind of protector could easily fall prey to violence or exploitation.

The lives of the poor were made harder by two crucial factors: the lack of work that paid enough to live on and the high price of even rudimentary accommodation. In most cities of the empire, accommodation was scarce and expensive. In Rome it was often prohibitively so. The average room at the top of a tenement block – so on the third floor of a poorly constructed *insula* – could have cost forty denarii a month. For a labourer earning one denarius a day, that was more than his monthly income – even assuming he got hired every day. The largest rooms in such blocks – the ones on the ground floor, especially – would have cost as much as 625 denarii a month. So, it's little wonder that most rooms were sublet and dangerously overcrowded. Often tenants would sleep in shifts, with those working at night sleeping through the day as best they could before rolling up their mats and making way for those who had worked through the day to come and sleep as they went off to do the night shift.

And there were always new arrivals seeking accommodation. One consequence of the empire's rapid expansion was that the cities attracted people of all kinds: merchants and artisans chasing work and markets, displaced peasants thinking they would find a better life in the city, runaway or freed slaves, refugees fleeing war and piracy, demobilized soldiers. These people with their families pressed into already overcrowded urban areas, bringing their languages, their customs, their diets, and their ways of settling scores into already volatile environments. No wonder contemporary writers looked anxiously at the cities' poor, fearful of being knifed or clubbed or caught up in a riot.

What language do you speak?

When Paul wrote to the collection of small gatherings meeting around Rome's poorer parts, he wrote in Greek because the followers of Jesus in that city were nearly all recent arrivals, outsiders in a city that spoke Latin. We see this in Romans 16 where, despite having never set foot in their city, he sends a series of greetings to friends, even family, who had migrated to Rome for a range of reasons in the AD 50s and were now part of the small communities of Jesus-followers in the city receiving a letter from the famous apostle.

The frequent riots in Rome had led to some of these people being expelled from the city for being trouble-makers. The Roman historians Tacitus and Suetonius tell us that Claudius expelled some Jews after rioting had broken out, stirred by someone called *Chrestus*. This is almost certainly a mispronunciation of the Greek name *Christos* and the authors are referring to disturbances that had broken out in the city's Jewish quarter between those who held Jesus of Nazareth to be the long-awaited Jewish Messiah (the Christ) and those Jews who disagreed.

Luke tells of one couple caught up in this. Priscilla and Aquila were tent-makers who had been expelled from Rome and had set up their business in Corinth, a port city awash with migrants from all over the empire. Paul on his arrival there in around AD 50, a year after Claudius's edict of expulsion, went looking for people he could work with (he too was a tent-maker or leather-worker) and he found this couple, who had already set up shop and were doing business in the city (Acts 18:1–3).

Paul sends greetings to this couple at the end of Romans. Clearly, after the heat had died down (and Claudius had died), they had been able to return to Rome and pick up the threads of their old life. But since Aquila is described as a native of Pontus, a province of what is now Turkey, it is clear that they were migrants in Rome, even if they increasingly viewed it as their home.

The same was almost certainly true of other cities where the Christian movement had a presence. In Antioch, for example, when Luke tells us about the leadership of the fledgling community, not one of the five named individuals is a native of the city. There is Paul from Tarsus, Barnabas from Cyprus, Simeon probably from Ethiopia (judging by his nickname), Lucius from what is now Libya, and Manaen, who was probably from Jerusalem but might have been from Rome (Acts 13:1–3).

The writing's on the wall

One feature of ancient cities that modern city-dwellers would find familiar is the presence of graffiti. What is more surprising is that being a graffiti artist in the Roman empire was a paid position.

It is Pompeii that has given us the clearest insight into this. All over the city, archaeologists have found graffiti of all kinds. This is both where you would expect it – on toilet walls, in brothels and inns – and also in rooms where children were obviously avoiding being educated, because scratched just above skirting-board level are comments about cruel and unsympathetic teachers. And there is a whole raft of scrawled comments on walls all over the city along the lines of "Sabinus was here".

Antioch

Antioch, the city where the followers of Jesus were first called "Christians" (Acts 11:26), was a bustling, cosmopolitan, vibrant, and violent place. A city with a population of around 250,000, it was a melting-pot of races and cultures because it stood on a key trade route between Palestine and Asia Minor.

It had been a Roman city since 64 BC and was settled with veterans of the legions as well as administrators who oversaw the collection of taxes and regulation of the many markets. By the first century it was seen as the third city of the empire after Rome and Alexandria.

There had been a Jewish population in the city for a couple of hundred years. The first settlers were not the usual merchants or people displaced by conflict, but veterans of the Seleucid army. Herod the Great had built a two-and-a-half-mile (4 km) colonnaded street that ran north to south in the centre of the city as testament to its importance as a centre of both Roman and Jewish life.

The Jewish community, probably numbering around 50,000, enjoyed various privileges. They were allowed to observe the sabbath and to keep their festivals and they were exempt from military service. This tended to make the community highly visible, however, and through the first century it was involved in various violent disturbances.

The worst of these happened in the late AD 30s when Caligula was emperor. Unrest in Judea led to a shrine to the emperor in the coastal city of Jamnia being torn down by disaffected Jews. In Antioch, where the Gentile citizens held Caligula and his father, Germanicus, in particularly high honour, riots broke out, synagogues were burned, and a good number of people on both sides of the ethnic divide were killed.

These tense times coincided with the arrival of the first Christians in the city. They were ordinary people fleeing north following the outbreak of violence against the churches in Jerusalem in the mid-30s (Acts 6:1 – 8:3). As they preached, Gentiles as well as Jews were attracted to the new movement (Acts 11:19–30).

Very quickly Antioch established itself as a key centre for the early Christians. The label "Christian" was coined in the city because the gatherings of Jesus-followers contained people from all the city's communities and not just Jews – this is clear from the church's leaders listed in Acts 13:1: there were individuals from Cyrene in North Africa, from Ethiopia, from Herod Antipas's court in Judea, from Tarsus, and from Cyprus.

This made Antioch pivotal in the development of the Christian movement. It was in this city over a meal, as Christians gathered to remember Jesus, that a dispute broke out as to whether Jews and Gentiles could eat at the same table. It led to a vital meeting taking place in Jerusalem probably around AD 48, which finally and forever opened the doors of the church to people from all nations (Galatians 2:11–14; Acts 15:1–35).

And from this city the first Christian missionaries were commissioned and sent (Acts 13:1–5). Until this time, the message had been passed on through casual conversation and chance meetings. Paul and Barnabas were sent by the Christians in Antioch specifically to preach the gospel and plant churches in other cities.

But it also appears that some people were paid to produce graffiti. It was the billboard advertising of the ancient city, announcing games and other entertainments, political meetings, and events at the theatres. One such artist in Pompeii was called Aemilius Celer, who wrote the following on a whitewashed wall in the city:

Twenty pairs of gladiators sponsored by Decimus Lucretius Satrius Valens, priest of Nero Caesar, and ten pairs of gladiators sponsored by his son, Decimus Lucretius Valens, will fight on 8, 9, 10, 11, and 12 April. A wild animal hunt will additionally be offered. The awnings will be employed. Aemilius Celer, alone in the moonlight, wrote this.

The artist marked his own home with a simple "Aemilius Celer lives here" and got involved in local politics, writing graffiti on behalf of candidates for various municipal posts. He even sought to protect his handiwork by writing underneath some of his graffiti: "if you deliberately deface this sign, may you fall seriously ill".

Mixing the classes

It used to be thought that there was a rigid social division in the cities, with the rich living in well-appointed walled houses on the edge of town, separated from the poor in the *insulae* in the crowded city centres. But this was not the case. The evidence suggests that the rich and poor lived in close proximity, often sharing the same apartment blocks. British archaeologist Andrew Wallace-Hadrill has undertaken a detailed study of one *insula* in Rome's Termini quarter with fascinating results.

Before taking a brief look, we need to understand the various ways in which the word *insula* is used. Originally, it seems, it was the term for the plot of land formed by the intersection of roads, what the Americans would call a "block". Depending on the size of the block, it could have several properties on it. It was also used by those gathering census data as a unit of property inhabited by a single household. Finally – and most commonly – the word is used to describe a type of building, an apartment block as distinct from a villa-style house (also called an atrium or peristyle *domus*). These types are discussed further in chapter 2.

Wallace-Hadrill suggests that close investigation of particular *insulae* in Rome, Ostia, and Pompeii reveals that it is better to talk about housefuls rather than households because the evidence suggests that what were once thought to be the dwelling-places of a single family (or household) turn out on closer inspection to have been home to several families, some linked by blood, others by finance (that is, they were commercial tenants of the family that owned and also lived in the *insula*).

What a close examination of the Termini quarter shows us is that in a tightly packed, compact location, breasting two roads, were a *domus*, a public bath-house, a magnificent hall (or *schola*) that could have been used for meetings, banquets, or theatrical productions, a twin row of shop-fronts that could have housed artisans making and selling manufactured goods, as well as *popinae* or *tavernae* selling food and drink. There is evidence that each of these structures had second and possibly third floors above them that would have formed apartments for tenants.

That this whole suite of buildings probably had a single owner is attested by the fact that there is common drainage and common features in the brickwork, suggesting that the whole site was put up at the same time. In short, it looks like a speculatively built mixed development, offering a variety of services as well as types of living accommodation.

It is almost certain, therefore, that quite well-off people lived cheek by jowl with poorer neighbours, that artisans lived and worked close by members of the elite who were independently wealthy (probably living off the rental income of farms in the Italian countryside), that distant members of the imperial household were near neighbours of merchants responsible for bringing grain or wine into the city through Ostia.

It suggests that Roman cities were clusters of mixed neighbourhoods where people of different social groups lived in close proximity. This means that, when we come to ask questions about the social location of the early followers of Jesus and where they met for meals and worship, it becomes harder to argue that they must have been either rich or poor and more likely that they were as mixed as the neighbourhoods in which they met.

In streets such as these

It was in this vibrant and volatile scene that the early Christian movement took root. In the backstreets of cities across the empire, small groups of men and women, mostly at the poorer end of the social spectrum, met over a simple dinner to talk about Jesus of Nazareth, to worship him and base their lives on his teaching and values.

As Pliny the Younger, the governor of Pontus and Bithynia – a Roman province in modern-day Turkey – observed of them:

. . . they met regularly on a fixed day before dawn to sing responsively a hymn to Christ as to a god, and to bind themselves by oath, not to some crime, but not to commit fraud, theft, or adultery, nor to falsify their trust, nor to refuse to return a deposit when called upon to do so. When this was over, it was their custom to depart and to reassemble later to take food – but ordinary, harmless food.

A Man of Privilege?

In the greetings at the end of his letter to the Romans, Paul mentions a man called Erastus. He describes him as the *oikonomos* of the city (of Corinth, where Paul is writing from). There has been a lot of debate among biblical scholars about what this term means and what it tells us about Erastus.

The Greek word means "steward" but clearly in the context that Paul uses it, it is a job title. The problem is that Corinth, though in Greece, was a Roman colony and therefore the offices of the city's hierarchy had Latin rather than Greek labels.

Recently archaeologists have been studying inscriptions found at another Roman colony in the province, the city of Patras, and have determined that the most likely Latin equivalent of the term *oikonomos* is quaestor.

If this is true, then it would have made Erastus a man of real substance and political clout. Quaestors were the men in the magistracy who had responsibility for making and receiving payments on behalf of the city's treasury. To hold such an office, they had to be Roman citizens and members of the local senatorial class (the decurions). They were also required to have personal wealth of 100,000 sesterces, making them among the 100 wealthiest men in the city.

So, if Erastus is indeed the quaestor of Corinth, it indicates that, even quite early on, the Christian movement was attracting men (and women) of high social standing. It was not just a movement of the urban poor. Such a finding has a bearing on the nature of the Christian gatherings and leadership within them, as well as the economic relationships between members. Chapter 7 will pick up some of these issues.

Who's in Charge Here?

Public administration in Rome was handled by a number of magistrates. These posts were filled by election by one's peers – that is, other members of the local elites – and were usually for one-year periods. At the bottom of this particular ladder were the quaestors, responsible for the city finances. They had to be independently wealthy men of at least thirty years of age.

Next came the aediles, responsible for urban infrastructure, such as major roads and water systems, and for ensuring that market-traders operated fairly. They also had a key role in putting on public festivals. Aediles had to be at least thirty-six years old. Next up were praetors, who had to be at least thirty-nine years old and were responsible for overseeing the law courts. At the top of this tree was the consulship. To be a consul you had to be at least forty-two years old. Elected for a year, they oversaw all the activities of the municipality. Most Roman cities across the empire followed this pattern of government.

Municipal offices were not paid posts as they are in modern bureaucracies. To be eligible to hold office, one had to have wealth and be prepared to spend it in order to get the job done. This is why statues and inscriptions across the empire laud the generosity of the men who held public office. It was their funds that paid for municipal buildings, temples, public squares, and the pavements that linked them all together.

CHAPTER 2

THE HOMES PEOPLE LIVED IN

So, the early Christians lived in cities. But what kind of homes did they live in? This question is not only interesting – after all, you only have to turn on the television to see how fascinated we are by people's homes – it is also essential for understanding their world. This is because the places where the first Christians lived were also the places where they worked (for the most part) and met for worship and learning. So understanding their physical location is crucial for gaining insight into their daily lives and social relationships.

It used to be thought that the few rich in the Roman empire lived in large, spacious, well-appointed villas while the poor masses huddled together in overcrowded, badly constructed apartment blocks, often with a whole family in a single room. There is a good deal of truth in this. But this simple picture has not survived the detailed work of archaeologists investigating the remains of living spaces across the empire, especially in Pompeii and Ostia, Corinth and Ephesus.

It seems that architectural styles were pretty limited in the ancient world. The two dominant housing designs are generally referred to as the *domus* and the *insula*. The *domus* was a villa-style house, usually constructed over one or two storeys around a central courtyard. The *insula* was a block of apartments, usually with shop-fronts at street level and multi-room living spaces on the floors above, getting smaller and more basic as they went up.

We will examine these two housing styles in some detail before looking at what the physical remains from the cities that have been substantially excavated tell us about the precise nature of living arrangements in the empire. The results of these studies are both fascinating and surprising and throw shafts of light on the nature of the early Christian communities that gathered in these cities.

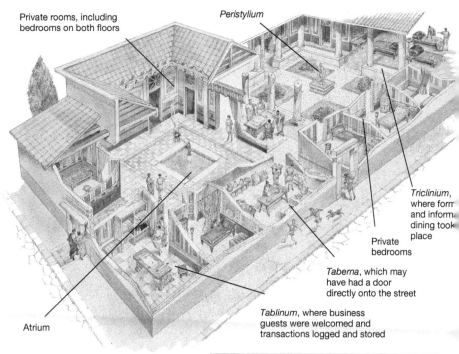

Private rooms, including bedrooms on both floors

Peristylium

Triclinium, where form and inform. dining took place

Private bedrooms

Taberna, which may have had a door directly onto the street

Tablinum, where business guests were welcomed and transactions logged and stored

Atrium

High-angle view of a residential building in Pompeii.

A Roman's home was his castle

Visitors to Pompeii often gasp when they walk into the houses left by the eruption, partly because they are so well preserved – though the colours on the walls have faded somewhat – but also because they can imagine living in them: their layout is very similar to housing across the world today. But that familiarity masks radical differences in the way the houses of the better off were laid out and what amenities they could boast.

The basic design was reproduced right across the ancient world. There is a detailed cross-sectional picture of a Roman *domus* above, to which you should refer while reading the following description.

A *domus* was accessed from the street by double doors set in a substantial brick wall. There were very few windows on the outside walls of properties for security and privacy reasons. In the absence of glass, which though available was not widely used even in the homes of the rich, such windows would have been just holes in the wall and would have let in any unwelcome element – both the weather and undesirable passers-by. Often the doorway was between shop-fronts that were an integral part of the house.

Going through the doors led into a narrow corridor called the *vestibulum*. The front doors of such houses – especially those owned and occupied by a single elite family – were opened at dawn and shut at sunset. This meant that the *vestibulum* was accessible to anyone who wanted to enter. For this reason, there was usually a household slave stationed in a small booth to ensure that only people with legitimate business in the house gained entrance – but it needs to be remembered that merely coming to look at the decoration might have been legitimate business, since it would enhance the status of the householder to have his taste admired by lots of people.

Standing in the *vestibulum* the visitor would be able to look into the heart of the house. At the end of the corridor were the *fauces*, the main doors that led into the atrium, which was an open courtyard, often with a well or pool that captured rain water at the centre, and with the main ground-floor rooms leading off it.

A visitor to a large house would have seen that beyond the atrium there was another courtyard area, usually surrounded by columns. This was the *peristylium* (often referred to as the peristyle in English), a colonnaded garden area at the rear of the property. Sometimes this garden was purely ornamental, offering shade and a pleasant environment in which family members could sit and sometimes work. But more often than not it was a place where fruit, olives, and vegetables were grown by the householder.

The *peristylium* was surrounded by rooms that were probably used as bedrooms, either for members of the family or for household slaves and retainers – depending on the numbers living in the home and whether there were rooms upstairs that the family could use. Such rooms, whether on the ground or first floor of the house, constituted the private part of the residence that was off-limits to all but family.

The internal walls of such a house would have been brightly decorated with bold murals of scenes from Greek and Roman mythology and wall-hangings and curtains of multicoloured fabric. Pottery and statues would also have adorned the spaces. All this would have been visible to the visitor standing in the *vestibulum* and was intended to impress them with the good taste and wealth of the householder who owned the property.

Welcome to dinner

In the rooms leading off the atrium the majority of day-time activities took place. In most homes there would have been a *triclinium*, a dining-room. The word literally means "three couches" and this indicates the traditional way in which triclinia were laid out. The formal dinners of well-to-do Romans took place with guests reclining on couches placed around three walls of the triclinium, three to a couch. This means that nine guests could eat comfortably, the food being served by household servants on small tables set at the centre of the room.

Of course, it is almost unthinkable that even in well-off homes every meal was taken in this way. Most meals were probably eaten in a variety of locations, sitting upright on a chair or a wall in the atrium or *peristylium*. Formal dinners, also known as symposia, were relatively rare events except in the homes of the very wealthy. But such meals might have been the model adopted by the early Christians for their worship services and celebration of the Lord's Supper (see chapter 4).

Open for business

Opposite the triclinium, leading off the atrium in the other direction, was another substantial room known as the *tablinum*. This was the main reception room of the home. The room might have been separated from the atrium and *peristylium* only by curtains or foldable wooden screens, allowing the space to be opened up when needed – for a celebration banquet or large gathering, for instance.

In this room the master of the house would receive visitors, often clients or business partners of one sort or another. Possibly in this room the master and his household slaves might have done any paperwork associated with the business of the household. It is here that he would have conducted any political business he was involved in, welcomed city officials, and planned civic functions or the banquets of any guild or association of which he might have been a member.

If the shop-fronts attached to the house were managed by the family that occupied the home, the *tablinum* could have been the place where orders were written up and records collated. Possibly in a substantial home there would have been another room where such records – on clay tablets or parchment rolls – would have been kept.

Behind the shop units was a room that was probably the kitchen. This would have been a small room with a hearth for a fire and an arrangement over it to allow pots and kettles to be put over the fire to heat. Meat, on the relatively rare occasions when it would be served, was almost certainly roasted on spits over braziers outside in the *peristylium*. The fact that kitchens were small meant that it was impossible to produce large banquets in them. But since the dining-room could only hold nine to a dozen people, the scale of catering was never anything but rudimentary except in the most prosperous homes of the elite.

Apartment living – Roman-style

Those who did not live in a *domus* – and were not living on the streets, in caves, among the tombs on the edge of town, or in makeshift shacks leaning against the sides of houses – lived in an apartment block or *insula*. These were less standard and so it is not possible to describe a typical flat.

Some were just rooms behind shop-fronts. Perhaps a shop or bar worker had a place to sleep and another place to prepare food behind the room where their business was conducted. Some shop and bar workers lived on mezzanine floors suspended above the shop, offering space for a sleeping mat but precious little else.

Other apartments were suites of rooms on the first or second floors above shops. Again there would have been rooms for the family to sleep in and a room in which to prepare and eat food and perhaps entertain guests. The better appointed *insulae* would have had a family lounge, off which all the other rooms led, where meals could be prepared and eaten. But often families – because of the difficulty of cooking in such an apartment – obtained their food at the corner *popina* and ate outside or back in their sleeping quarters. On the top floors of such blocks, the poorest families rented single rooms where they ate and slept in utterly basic conditions. They probably had no furniture to speak of, sleeping on mats, and obtaining food from street vendors, which they ate with their hands.

Floor space in the *insulae* was at a premium in the early years of the empire because laws limited the height of buildings to 50 feet – though the regulations were frequently flouted. It was also limited by the fact that *insulae* were usually built around a central courtyard. This was to ensure light got into most rooms and to allow access to the shared amenities – mainly water, probably in the form of a well or a fountain in the centre of the courtyard, and a latrine, where waste of all kinds would be flushed into a cesspit. The better-built *insulae* had a latrine on each floor and chutes for waste disposal – but these were rare in the first century.

While a *domus* owned and occupied by a rich family would have been attractively decorated, with mosaics on the floors, paintings on the walls, and highly coloured fabrics used to divide up living spaces, the *insulae* would have been very bare in comparison. They were built of brick or plastered stucco with mud or brick floors. Many blocks were made of wood and mud-brick, which made them insecure and prone to burn down. Building standards gradually improved during the first century but the poor still lived in substandard, overcrowded accommodation at the end of the first Christian century as they did at its beginning.

While many *domus*-style homes had heating in the form of fireplaces in some of the rooms and even underfloor heating such as was used in the bath-houses (see pp. 42–43), the *insulae* lacked heating of any kind. There were no fireplaces and the absence of glass in the windows meant that they could be very cold indeed. Some residents lit braziers in the common areas of the blocks and used them for cooking as well as heating. At night they would have been lit by oil lamps. All these naked flames added to the risk of fire, and *insulae* frequently burned down.

Indeed the poor quality of many *insulae* is highlighted by the satirist Juvenal, who mused:

who at cool Praeneste or at Volsinii amid its leafy hills, was ever afraid of his house tumbling down? But here we inhabit a city propped up for the most part by slats; for that is how the landlord patches up the crack in the old wall, bidding the inmates sleep at ease under the ruin that hangs above their heads.

He was probably overstating the case, but there is evidence of frequent building collapses in Rome through the first century. And it is likely that other cities had similar stories to tell.

In Rome there were twenty-five apartment blocks for every single *domus*-style house. A fourth-century record informs us that the respective figures were 46,602 and 1,797. As other cities grew, the proportions were probably the same. The blocks were thrown up to meet the rising demand for accommodation as people flowed into the cities drawn by the promise of a better life than the one they were leading in the countryside.

At street level, the *insulae* were continuous rows of small shops (*tabernae*). During the day these shops were open to the world; at night they would have been closed up with heavy wooden shutters. The shops would have been retail outlets, selling a wide variety of goods, and workshops where artisans and craft-workers made products to order and for sale. These would have been noisy, smelly places interspersed with *popinae* where food and drink were on sale all day.

When the shops shut for the night, the noise would not have died down, just changed. After dark, carts, banned from the streets during daylight hours because of congestion, were allowed to roam the city, delivering and collecting goods. And in most cities there was a vibrant and noisy night-life featuring the usual suspects – groups of young men out drinking, prostitutes looking for business, people going to and from dinner parties – as well as large numbers of *insula*-dwellers who had worked through the day and needed, once it was too dark to work, to get water, find food, and perhaps unwind after a day bent over a loom, anvil, or bench.

I work here as well

It is important to bear in mind when we think about housing that this was not only where people lived but also where most people worked. Obviously, household slaves worked where they lived, keeping the household running, serving as cooks, maids, porters, gardeners, etc. Equally obviously, if those who occupied a *domus* owned and managed the shops at the front of the house, members of the family and not just slaves would have worked out of them.

But it is also the case that many of the things that in the modern world are bought from third parties, in the ancient world were made at home. So in most homes, for example, families would have made their own clothes. In the villas of the better off, looms would have been set up in the atria for weaving cloth for decorative purposes as well as making and mending clothes. But even in the homes of the poor, clothes would have been made or, more likely, mended and made to last another season by a member of the family.

And families whose income was based on making and selling a product would have undertaken all the manufacturing in their home. So, for instance, a baker would have milled his flour and moulded and baked his loaves in his home, housing the equipment needed for the purpose around his living space. A family that earned its living by making the everyday pots that people needed for cooking and eating would, similarly, have housed the potter's wheels and kilns needed for such a trade in their home and sold the goods they made through a *taberna* at the front of either the *domus* or *insula* in which they lived.

Families, which for all but the poorest in society meant not just parents and children but also surviving grandparents, uncles, aunts, and cousins, along with any slaves the family owned, would have lived and worked in the same space. For this reason, their homes would have been open to the public in the sense that customers and suppliers of raw materials would have been coming and going throughout the day and sometimes well into the evening.

Mixed-housing schemes

But even this does not tell the whole story about urban living in the first century. In the previous chapter we saw how careful examination of a single *insula* reveals that a variety of households would have lived in close proximity. This is important not only for understanding where and how people lived but also for how to make sense of what we read in the New Testament about the way early churches were organized.

So, for instance, in the "*insula* of the Menander" in Pompeii, archaeologists have discovered a number of individual homes of various sizes and types that shared common amenities, such as water and drainage. The site contains a really enormous *domus*, with a stable yard and huge *peristylium*. But this is surrounded by dwellings of various shapes and styles.

A tiny house of one or possibly two rooms, which opens on the street, appears to have been occupied by a stonemason. Not far away, a much larger house was the home and workshop of a cabinet-maker. On one corner of the plot, there was a *popina*. On the site there was a bath-house which would have had a number of slaves working at it, whose poor single-room accommodation has also been identified.

Some scholars have sought to rate people's position on the social and economic ladder by assessing the floor area of their living accommodation. So the stonemason lived in a home of 40 square metres, whereas the cabinet-maker's home was some 310 square metres, and the substantial house at the centre of the property enjoyed 1,700 square metres. The suggestion is that the more space you occupied, the higher up the social scale you were likely to be.

But the issue is not just how much space people had but the fact that they lived so close to each other, almost to the point of having front doors next to each other off the same street.

The other factor that brought people into close proximity was that the upstairs rooms of a *domus* were often let out to other families. Just because someone lived in a *domus*, it did not mean that they were wealthy. Only the elite minority owned property – with a few exceptions; everyone else, even those living in *domi*, rented. Possibly for many people in cities, the only way they could balance the budget was to let out parts of the property they lived in to another family. Often these people would share the same front door as the owners of the house but there is evidence in a lot of sites of external stairs being added to allow tenants independent access.

Finally, it is worth bearing in mind that many wealthy people chose to buy or rent an apartment in a well-sited *insula* in the city because their main residence was in the country. Many elite families would have needed to have a base in Rome, or the commercial centre nearest to where their family farm and principal residence was located.

Meeting the neighbours

It was the close proximity of people in the cities that gave the early Christians a ready audience for their message. The two places where people were most likely to meet were at work or at a meal. Since these were often in the same place, it meant that people saw each other often.

Acts 18:7 tells us about the house of Titius Justus where Paul stayed. Scholars believe that this man is also known as Gaius and is the same as the Gaius referred to in Romans 16:23. As an early believer in the city he played a significant role in the development of the church – not least because he appears to have had a house large enough to accommodate a lot of people.

Chapter 3 will discuss how workplace encounters were the primary way in which the early Christians transmitted their message through the cities of the empire. But it does not need much imagination to think of Paul, Aquila, and Priscilla at the end of the working day, getting food at the *popina* on the corner of the *insula* where their workshop was and engaging in conversation with others eating and drinking there. It is likely that orders for tents or other leather goods resulted in invitations to people's homes to deliver what had been made, and that conversations there led to dinner invitations and new churches forming in the homes of people drawn to the new faith.

Christians did not meet in special buildings called "churches" for at least 200 years. So the worship life of the early Christians happened in the homes where they lived. This meant that groups of believers might gather either in the *domus* belonging to – or rented by – one of the few wealthier Christians in Corinth or Ephesus or Rome, or in one of the *insulae* where the majority lived. It is possible to think of small huddles of people eating a shared meal in a workshop or courtyard, telling the stories of Jesus to one another and to any interested bystanders who happened to stop by, drawn as much by the food, no doubt, as by the laughter and intense conversation.

Bath time

If people know one thing about the Romans it is that they invented the public bath – though this is not strictly true. They took it over from the Greeks but they developed it in such a way that the baths became synonymous with Roman culture. Everywhere the legions went, the baths went with them.

One obvious reason for the development of public baths was that most homes, whether large or small, inhabited by rich or poor, did not have bathing facilities. So for anything more than a sponge down at a fountain or basin, a visit to the public baths was essential.

But the baths were so much more than a place to get a wash. They were a social centre, a place to gather and meet friends, and an escape

Ephesus

The city of Ephesus grew up around its most famous landmark, the temple of Artemis. And, as it reached its golden years as the largest city in Asia Minor, it was more and more dependent on tourism and pilgrimage, making the arrival of Christians particularly unwelcome.

There had been a settlement in the valley that straddled the river Cayster as it flowed into the Aegean Sea for at least a thousand years before the Roman empire rose to the west of it. For half a millennium it had been the centre of the worship of Artemis.

The Greek empire of Alexander took control of the city and moved it from around Artemis's temple, rebuilding it around the harbour that was the first reason for its prosperity. Ships brought grain from Egypt for the surrounding towns and villages and took away manufactured goods, cloth, and dyes from the workshops of Asia Minor.

By the first century this trade was declining because the harbour was silting up. But the prosperity of Ephesus was not waning. It was a magnet for pilgrims and a centre of banking – and both depended on the temple of Artemis.

Described as one of the seven wonders of the world, the temple stood in the hills above the city on 127 marble columns. Facing west to catch the setting sun, its evening rituals in honour of the goddess of fertility attracted thousands of devotees. And those devotees, who came from near and far, bought goods and trinkets sold in her honour, swelling the treasury that stood in the temple and formed the basis of a banking centre.

The philosopher Dio Chrysostom exclaimed that even kings "deposit there in order that it may be safe, since no one has ever dared to violate that place". His assessment was not strictly accurate since Julius Caesar helped himself from its coffers and some of his successors followed suit!

The Romans made it their provincial capital and thus a centre for legal, political, and commercial business. It boasted a 25,000-seat theatre, which stood at the end of a colonnaded street rising up from the harbour. It had a substantial *agora*, an outdoor market, that was a centre for the buying and selling of local produce and manufactures.

But at the core of its prosperity was the cult of Artemis or Diana. Her temple, built and rebuilt since the sixth century BC, was a centre of worship and magic that drew people from all over the empire to worship and be initiated in its arts so that they could go back to their homes to establish associations in her name.

The apostle Paul arrived in Ephesus in around AD 52, fresh from a prolonged and successful stay in Corinth. Luke tells us that he stayed for over two years. During this time he spoke both in the local synagogue and for a longer period in a hall that belonged to the wonderfully named Tyrannus (Acts 19:8–10). Perhaps he behaved like a visiting philosopher, giving lectures there at the end of the working day since it is likely that Paul and his team needed to work to support themselves.

The success of the mission resulted in a clash with those who earned their living from the city's traditional religious allegiances. Luke tells us that several converts had been practitioners of magic and that, as a result of their new-found faith, they burned all their old books (Acts 19:18–19).

He also tells us about a riot instigated by Demetrius, a silversmith, who felt that his livelihood was being threatened by this new cult. He reasoned that if people followed Jesus, they would not buy the artefacts he sold that aided their worship of Artemis. There is a lively account of the exchange that took place in Acts 19:23–41.

The church seems to have weathered such storms, since the city was a centre of Christianity for at least 500 years before it was gradually abandoned in the wake of the fall of the Roman empire. It is now one of the greatest archaeological sites in the world.

from the bleakness of most people's apartments. Some baths had exercise rooms, beauty parlours, even libraries.

Turning the heat up

At the heart of the Roman baths was a suite of rooms kept at different temperatures. Historians differ on the order in which the rooms were meant to be visited, and probably there was no rule that said you had to go from hot to cold or vice versa. In the room with hot water – the *calidarium* – bathers would splash themselves with water and use scrapers to remove the dirt (sometimes having first applied olive oil to their skin). The rich would often bring a slave to perform this task; some baths had employees (also slaves) on hand to scrape lone bathers; sometimes you had to do it yourself.

In many public baths, the sexes were separated, but in some there was mixed bathing, so some baths got a reputation for being morally suspect. One public bath in Pompeii has a changing room with a frieze showing couples and groups enjoying sexual intercourse, which has led some historians to speculate the baths also operated as a brothel. But this was probably an exception.

The baths seem to have been places where people – mainly those with some disposable income (though most public baths were free to use or charged only a nominal entrance fee) – met, got clean, took a bit of exercise, chewed the fat, and did business or political deals. The writer Seneca, whose apartment was above a public bath complex, found it a less than relaxing experience:

The whack of the masseur's hand, the grunts of the gymnast as he swung his dumb-bells, the splashing of the swimmer, the roars of the man who sang as he bathed, the yelps of the man who was having his armpits depilated, and the cries of sellers of sausage, cakes, and other goodies . . .

It all meant that he was as disturbed by the constant din from the baths below his flat as he was by the noises on the streets outside.

Places of innovation

The baths were among the notable feats of Roman engineering. Not only did their proliferation mean that city engineers had to build aqueducts to bring a constant supply of fresh water into the city, but they also had to devise a system for heating that water. They did this by an underfloor heating system known as a "hypocaust". A furnace in the basement heated air that was circulated in ducts underneath floors that were raised on piles of tiles. The rooms nearest the furnace were the hottest. The system worked well enough for it to be transferred to the homes of the wealthy to provide them with a form of central heating.

Whether anyone got clean in the baths is a moot point, however. The water was changed infrequently, there was no chlorination to remove impurities, bodily secretions of all kinds – including large quantities of urine – would build up through the day, and the water would be polluted by olive oil and skin cells from the vigorous scraping that went on in the *calidarium*.

Given how important bathing was to Roman culture, it is surprising that we have no record of Paul or any other early Christian visiting the baths; nowhere in the early Christian writings is there reference to them. This means either that they were a common part of life – like eating and sleeping – and did not require comment, or that they were not a feature of the lives of the majority of Christians, who were generally poor, had to work in the hours of daylight, and therefore did not have the leisure time or disposable income required to enjoy the baths to their full.

Finding our way around Corinth

An understanding of where and how people lived in the Roman empire is essential for grasping some features of the early Christian writings. Here and in a number of subsequent chapters we will look at how an accurate picture of the world of the early church helps us to read 1 Corinthians, a letter sent by the apostle Paul to a group of Christians in the Roman colony of Corinth sometime in the mid-50s AD.

The first thing to notice is that Paul writes about a number of households that were probably hosts to groups of believers. There was no single church in Corinth, although from time to time it seems that a man called Gaius was able to entertain all the believers in his home. Normally the believers met in various homes dotted around the city.

We have information about one or two of them and, based on knowledge about the way people lived from studies in other cities as well as Corinth, it is possible to build up a picture of what those households were like. Unfortunately, unlike in Pompeii, Ostia, and Rome, a complete Corinthian *insula* has yet to be excavated but what we know of the city from other sources suggests that its housing stock was every bit as mixed as all the other Roman cities.

So, it is likely that in the Corinthian port city of Cenchrea, where Phoebe (mentioned in Romans 16:1–2) lived, there would have been a mixture of *insula* and *domus* housing, just as in the port city of Ostia. Phoebe's business could have run from either style of dwelling but the fact that she travelled (she probably took Paul's letter from Corinth to Rome) and lived in a port city means that she was probably involved in the shipping industry in some way, and therefore might well have lived in an *insula* near the docks with business premises on the ground floor and an apartment above it.

Gaius, mentioned in Romans 16:23, along with Erastus, probably lived in a *domus* somewhere in the main city, given the fact that he is said to have been able to host the whole church, which probably then numbered between 100 and 120. It is highly unlikely that those sort of numbers could have fitted into an upstairs room in an apartment – even a big one.

Chloe is mentioned in 1 Corinthians 1:11. It is her people who have travelled to Ephesus from where Paul is writing to bring news of what is happening in the church. It is very unlikely that visiting Paul was the sole reason for their journey – that would suggest that they were pretty well off. Probably Chloe's household was engaged in some kind of business that necessitated travel to places such as Ephesus. It is interesting that it is Chloe who is named, not her husband, indicating that she was either a widow or had never married, an unusual state of affairs in the first century. The reference to "her people" probably means that those who visited Paul were household slaves who assisted in the running of whatever business Chloe was engaged in. If she was a craft-worker of some kind, she could well have lived in a small house with a *taberna* at the front or in an *insula*, working out of the ground floor and living above it. It is likely that her household had more than three people in it because, if she sent at least two to Ephesus, there must have been others back in Corinth to carry on the business.

It is suggested that she might have hosted a house church, a group of twenty or so Christians who gathered on a regular basis to worship, learn, and celebrate the Lord's Supper together.

The other household that Paul mentions is that of Stephanas (1 Corinthians 1:16; 16:15–18). Although Paul tells his hearers in Corinth to emulate Stephanas because of his service to the believers in the city, we are not told very much about him. The fact that he had a household does not mean that he was particularly wealthy, just that he did not live alone. Again it is likely that he was a craft-worker of some kind who lived by small-scale manufacturing undertaken by himself and either slaves or members of his family. So again it is likely that he would have lived in a small *domus* or *insula* apartment with a *taberna* from which to conduct his business.

The final couple we know were in Corinth are Aquila and Priscilla. Paul met this couple on his arrival in the city (Acts 18:1–3). They were tent-makers by trade, as Paul was himself, and they clearly travelled quite a bit, as we meet them in the New Testament not only in Corinth but also in Ephesus and Rome, while Luke tells us in Acts that Aquila originally came from Pontus in what is now Turkey.

It is quite likely that on arrival in Corinth in around AD 49–50, they rented a workshop with living accommodation so they could work as tent-makers. Corinth was a good place for them because every two years it hosted the Isthmian games, meaning there was good demand for tents and awnings. In Romans 16:3–5, after the couple had relocated to the capital, Paul greets them and the church in their home. The likelihood is that, as in Corinth and Ephesus, Aquila and Priscilla had hosted a gathering of Christians in their workshop or apartment.

That the church gathered in *insula* apartments is clear from the story of Eutychus that Luke tells us in Acts 20:7–12. Paul is in Troas. It is the night before he intends to set sail for Assos on his way ultimately to Jerusalem. Paul is speaking and has clearly been going on for quite a long time. The upstairs room he is in is pretty full because people are using up all the available space, including the window ledges. The length of the sermon and the heat generated by all the bodies in the room and the

Household Effects

Homes in the empire were sparsely furnished. Except in the houses of the super-rich, the elite 1 or 2 per cent of society, most dwellings would not have had much in them by way of fixtures and fittings.

The bedrooms might have had a wooden bed with a mattress, but a sleeping mat on the floor is more likely. There might have been one or two chairs in the reception room as well as the couches in the dining-rooms and a few soft furnishings, such as cushions and curtains around the ground floor.

Many of the pottery pieces on display in the atrium were everyday crockery items, used to serve food on when there were guests for dinner. Other items of crockery – the everyday and special plates used for eating – were stored in chests or cupboards, along with cutlery, although Romans only had spoons and knives – the fork would not be invented for a few centuries yet.

This means that household slaves and servants were frequently in the atrium gathering items needed for meals they were preparing. They would have to come to the atrium to collect water, as the house's own water supply was there.

It also seems that Roman kitchens, even in the homes of the wealthy, were not particularly well equipped. There were not enough pots and pans to prepare a number of dishes. Indeed, among the most frequent finds in the kitchens of Pompeii are flat dishes, burned on the bottom, and small shallow braziers, suggesting that a good deal of the food was barbecued at the table rather than cooked in the kitchen.

Many items in a Roman house would have been work-related. So there might be looms or potter's wheels in the atrium, ovens at the back of the property for baking bread or preparing meat for a *popina*, a table in the reception room where cloth could be measured and cut, or dried foodstuffs weighed and packaged.

So an atrium would be a bustling place, with visitors coming and going, family members conducting business or meeting friends, and slaves working away keeping the household fed and watered. This part of a home was anything but private.

Of course, life in an *insula* was different. People would gather in the central courtyard to collect water and probably to prepare food rather

> than in the apartment itself. Furnishing in such places was even more spartan than in a *domus*, the most common items being oil lamps – of which there would have been lots because it took a good number of them to light even a small room – and a cheap plate for each family member to eat off. The poorest apartments would have no furniture at all save a bedroll for sleeping on.

oil lamps needed for people to see mean that poor Eutychus falls asleep and out of the window. Luke tells us he fell three floors to his death (though Paul raised him up), probably into the *insula's* central courtyard. After they had all rushed down to check on Eutychus's health, Luke tells us they went back upstairs and broke bread; that is, they had a meal together.

So here is a snapshot of the early Christians worshipping, learning, and sharing food together in an ordinary apartment in an *insula* in downtown Troas, a scene that became increasingly common across the empire as the century unfolded.

CHAPTER 3

ALL IN A DAY'S WORK

The streets of Roman cities were busy, bustling, noisy places. Juvenal gives us a flavour of what it was like trying to get from A to B:

Though we hurry, we merely crawl; we're blocked by a surging mass ahead, a pushing wall of people behind. A man jabs me, elbowing through, one socks a chair pole against me, one cracks my skull with a beam, one knocks a wine cask against my ear. My legs are caked with splashing mud, from all sides the weight of enormous feet comes smashing on mine, and a soldier stamps his hobnails through to my sole.

Allowing for some artistic licence, he paints a vivid picture of streets thronging with activity, of buyers and sellers bartering over goods, of countless deliveries to and from numerous small shops and cafés, of sole traders hawking goods on a street corner, of messengers scurrying between the homes of the elite, of rich women being carried through the streets on litters, of wealthy civic leaders being followed by a sea of flunkies and retainers, of beggars, prostitutes, and street entertainers. Everywhere you looked someone was trying to get somewhere and earn a crust.

Living off the land

About 80 per cent of the empire's population earned their living through agriculture. Many scraped by as tenant farmers on smallholdings producing just enough to feed themselves and their families in the good years. Many more were slaves and day labourers on the large commercial farms of the aristocratic elite.

Even a good number of urban people worked on farms beyond the city gates. Each day they would walk to their fields to grow crops for themselves and the local market (if times were good). Some of these people – as the evidence from Pompeii in particular attests – were moderately prosperous, which is to say that they grew enough to feed their immediate family and have a surplus to sell that funded the purchase of tools and other necessities, as well as a few little luxuries. A tiny number made a really good living. But probably the majority, who did not own the land they worked, scraped out a meagre existence.

Most land was owned by the few aristocratic elite families, the senatorial and other ruling orders (see chapter 5), and formed the basis of their vast wealth. It was the aristocratic ideal not to work. Indeed it was felt to be degrading for people to have to work with their hands; that was the lot of slaves. So while an elite gentleman farmer might take an interest in crop rotation and grape varieties – in order to maximize the return from his estates – he would never be seen on the business end of a plough.

And they did not get directly involved in other kinds of business either. Indeed, an imperial decree from the first century, the *lex Claudia*, ruled it illegal for senators or their sons to own large merchant ships, the kind that were used to ship grain and other goods across the Mediterranean. But there is ample evidence that the more enterprising members of the elite got around this law by setting up a business in the name of a slave or more commonly a freedman (one of their former slaves). So while maintaining the illusion of aristocratic indolence, they were in fact growing even wealthier on the burgeoning trade associated with feeding the city of Rome and other cities of the empire through the first century.

One wonders if it might have been such people that the apostle Paul had in mind when he wrote to the small gathering of believers in Thessalonica that "anyone unwilling to work should not eat" (2 Thessalonians 3:10; more of this later).

Of course, the elite were not totally idle. Many of them worked as lawyers and as elected officials in the administration of the empire's cities; some of them, such as Juvenal, Seneca, and Pliny the Elder, combined such roles with writing and philosophy. But they received no payment for these jobs. They gave their services free as was fitting for men of their rank. Indeed, to hold most elected government offices you had to have substantial wealth at your disposal to discharge your duties.

For example, the man who held the office of curator of the grain supply was responsible for ensuring that sufficient grain came into the city to meet the population's needs, even in times of shortage and high prices. So, from time to time this involved buying large quantities of grain from abroad at his own expense and selling it at a lower price in the city for which he was responsible. The pattern for this was set by the emperor Augustus himself, who in 22 BC assumed the role for the city of Rome and testified in the *Res Gestae* (his account of the benefits of his reign) that "I delivered the whole city from apprehension [over grain shortages] and immediate danger at my own cost and by my own efforts". Such accounts, albeit less grand, can be found in cities all over the empire.

The long day dawns

But most people had to work or they certainly would not eat. Somewhere around a fifth of the empire's overall population were slaves – the proportion varied from region to region – chattels, wholly owned by their masters for the sole purpose of being put to work. This has led many historians to refer to the Roman economy as a slave economy. And it is undoubtedly true that slaves made up a large proportion of the rural workforce. There is ample archaeological evidence of chain gangs being set to work on the land on the larger estates in Roman Italy, made up of captured enemies or felons of one sort or another serving their punishment as bonded labourers.

But while slaves were an important part of the urban workforce, there were vastly more free people offering their labour and seeking to make a living on the busy streets.

The working day for most began before sunrise and lasted long after dusk. In elite households, slaves would rise while it was still dark to light fires, draw water, sweep and clean courtyards and the public spaces of the house, start preparing food (including baking or going to buy bread for breakfast), and open the house's front door for the first visit of clients (the so-called *salutatio*: see the next chapter). Through the day these household slaves would be meeting the needs of family members, serving food, helping them dress, running errands, washing clothes, carrying them on litters, receiving guests, cleaning up after them, and a thousand and one other duties. Very rich households had large numbers of slaves doing this kind of work.

Living hand to mouth

More modest homes also stirred early. Family members, possibly a slave or two, maybe a freed person who worked in the family's trade, would have to get ready for the day as the sun was breaking the horizon. Food would be prepared, fires lit in the kitchen. If the home was occupied by a craft-worker of some kind – a carpenter, cabinet-maker, potter, artist, statue-maker, jeweller, metalworker, tent-maker, and the like – the workshop had to be prepared for the day's work. Some craft-workers slept where they worked, so bedrolls would have to be put away and tools readied for the business of the day. Breakfast would have to be made or bought at the local *popina* and brought back to the home.

At the end of the working day, when the setting sun meant that it was too dark to see well enough to work in their ill-lit rooms (the oil lamps being quite inadequate), such craft-workers would clear up their tools, maybe deliver what they had been making through the day to customers, or send a messenger (perhaps a child or slave) to gather any orders for tomorrow's work.

Meanwhile, in the homes of the elite, dinner was in full swing in the triclinium. Diners would have gathered since the middle of the afternoon for a meal that could last four or five hours, with entertainment to follow. Perhaps such entertainment involved travelling musicians, dancers, or conjurors, hired for an hour or two as an after-dinner diversion. Perhaps lewder fare was on offer. Slaves would come and go with food courses and wine until well after dark. Then, guests would be met by members of their respective households – again, most likely slaves or loyal freedmen – who arrived with torches and clubs to guard their masters and mistresses (often carried on litters) on the journey back to their house across the city.

Say a little prayer for me

All through the day temples and shrines would have been open for worshippers. As explained in chapter 8, religion was everywhere in the cities of the empire. People were employed as priests to conduct sacrifices and receive offerings from those who came to worship. Often employment meant that they conducted rituals in return for meals and a place to sleep. They were on hand to assist the members of elite families who assumed the roles of senior religious leaders in the city.

The temples were also home to augurs, prophets, and soothsayers of all kinds, who were paid by people wanting to know their futures, seeking assurance that the auspices were good for a business deal or travel plans, or invoking a curse on a rival or lover who had jilted them. Some fortune-tellers plied their trade from bar to bar, of course, offering cheaper predictions than their temple counterparts.

Muscle for hire

While some workers in Rome's cities were skilled in various ways, including being able to read and write and therefore able to work as clerks, secretaries, even teachers, in richer households and businesses, many had only their muscle to offer a potential employer.

But there was considerable demand for such people. Throughout the first century many Roman cities, not just the capital, enjoyed a building boom. And construction sites needed thousands of willing hands. Whole armies of men were employed to dig out by hand the foundations of grand buildings, to carry vast supplies of building sand and gravel, brick, marble, and stone from wagons and barges onto the site, and to mix cement and concrete *in situ*. On one project, the emperor Claudius employed 30,000 men as diggers for eleven years.

Of course, building work came and went. Many of these casual labourers, who would have been paid a daily rate sufficient to buy food and possibly accommodation, endured frequent bouts of enforced idleness because of bad weather, injury, or the end of a particular project.

At the docks in Ostia, Puteoli, Cenchrea, and elsewhere, muscle was always needed to unload cargoes and transfer them onto carts and barges for onward travel. Many men would be needed to accompany cargoes from ships to their final destinations on donkey-carts or more likely by hand. This work was seasonal, however, as the big trading ships only sailed from the late spring to early autumn. Winter months would be lean for thousands of dock-workers and porters.

And in the cities themselves, there was plenty of work for men willing to carry things, anything from goods made in a workshop to statues bought for a grand house, from flour for a baker to cloth for a dressmaker. By and large, the transport industry consisted of men with muscles during the day and donkey-carts at night (these were not allowed on the streets of many cities during the day because of the congestion).

And at the bottom of the urban food chain, there was always a need for a man with a bucket to clear up after everyone else. Some were employed by the city to do so, others took the initiative and sought to sell what they collected as manure to smallholders and gardeners nearby.

The working week was seven days long. No one had a day off in the empire except Jewish people, who observed the sabbath, a complete day off work, on Saturdays. They were unique in this and the habit would have put even more pressure on most poor Jewish people in the cities, since the rule of thumb was that if you did not work that day, you would not eat that day, as most workers only earned enough to get them through the next twenty-four hours.

Trading on their skills

Many of the people mentioned in the New Testament were craft-workers or traders, trying to keep body and soul together in the urban mêlée.

Lydia, a native of Thyatira in Roman Asia Minor (modern-day Turkey), is described as a trader in purple. Paul meets her at Philippi, according to Acts 16:14–15. She is interesting for a number of reasons, the first of which is that she is a woman in a man's world.

All but the richest of women had to work, but they generally worked at home. They all had to do the domestic chores that any home needs to have done. So in ancient Roman cities we see women cooking, making and mending clothes, cleaning, and looking after children just as we do across our world today. In many ways this was where a Roman woman was meant to find her identity, and within the home – subject to her husband, the head of the family (as explored in chapter 6) – a wife had a certain degree of power and autonomy.

In homes where the main source of income came from the clothing trade, such women played an important role in overseeing spinning, weaving, sewing, and dyeing of cloth for making into garments. In many ways this was simply an extension of their domestic duties in a way that generated income for the household.

Other work roles for women included becoming midwives, wet-nurses, and personal attendants to elite women who lived nearby, again an extension of their child-rearing and domestic roles within the family.

Some women made a living as singers and dancers, bar workers, and entertainers of other kinds. These professions were seen as being of extremely low status and it was assumed that any woman engaging in them was available for sex – with or without payment. Indeed, women who worked in bars – often the slaves of the bar owner – were exempted from prosecution for adultery on the assumption that chastity could not be expected of them.

Women of substance

But from early in the reign of Augustus, more and more women emerged into the market-place, working alongside their husbands or even on their own account in a range of commercial activities.

Lydia of Philippi was one such woman. It is clear from Luke's account in Acts 16 that she was a single woman with a household. This means that she was either a widow whose husband had brought the family business to Philippi and then died – not uncommon in the first century – or that she was the single daughter of a Thyatiran purple merchant who had been sent to establish a base of operations in the important trading city of Philippi. The former is more likely.

The clothing industry was enjoying something of a boom in the first century. Demand was high and good-quality clothes were expensive; therefore those involved in their manufacture and marketing could earn a good living. Many women worked in the industry because of the domestic nature of clothes production: spinning, weaving, sewing, and making up the finished garments were all jobs that happened in ordinary family homes, using a handful of people, often slaves, in the manufacturing process.

Lydia's business was supplying a crucial ingredient to the upmarket end of the fashion business. The sale of purple dye was lucrative because purple was the colour of rank. Indeed, there were some purple dyes – the very best-quality ones – of which the manufacture and distribution were an imperial monopoly. But even those selling the more ordinary products stood to make a good living.

The wearing of purple clothes was strictly controlled, but it is clear that anyone in the empire aspiring to get noticed added a bit of purple to their look. In particular, dining-room furnishings were often purple – throws for couches, wall-hangings, and curtains – so the aspiring could impress their dinner guests.

Thyatira was a centre of the dyeing industry and in particular a major source of good-quality purple dyes. That is where Lydia had come from, where she had learned her trade and probably established her business or possibly inherited it from a dead husband or father.

We do not know if she had come to Philippi permanently or was only in the city for a while – perhaps to get the business established or to oversee a particularly important order – or if she came and went and travelled to other locations in pursuit of business. What we do know is that she is not mentioned in the letter Paul wrote to the church a few years after the visit Luke records in Acts 16. Perhaps by then she had returned to Thyatira or moved on to another city. It is entirely possible that she had died, since life was uncertain and short in the first century.

But when Paul arrived in Philippi, Lydia was doing well enough from her business to have a household that could accommodate three or four guests (Paul, Timothy, Silas, and Luke himself: Acts 16:15) and which became the centre of the small church that formed as a result of Paul's preaching (Acts 16:40).

Here we have an example of a single woman, living as a merchant with a household that could have consisted of any children she had, maybe her elderly parents and any slaves or employees associated with the business. There is no evidence, however, that she lived in a big house or that she was extremely wealthy. She was probably doing all right, living comfortably enough, generating sufficient income from her business to offer hospitality.

Transferable skills

Aquila and Priscilla were craft-workers, able to take their skills wherever they were needed. We meet them in Acts 18:1–3. It is about AD 50 and they have had to leave Rome, as the emperor Claudius has expelled some leaders in the Roman Jewish community because of disturbances over differing religious opinions.

As we have seen, the Roman historians Tacitus and Suetonius both tell us that these disturbances in AD 49 were instigated by one *Chrestus*, almost certainly a Latin misrendering of the Greek *Christos*. The trouble within the Jewish community was between those who believed Jesus to be the Jewish messiah and those who did not. The account in Acts tells us that such a situation is entirely likely, as Paul and his colleagues were frequently caught up in trouble at the synagogue because of their preaching. Claudius seems to have expelled the ringleaders on both sides and Aquila and Priscilla had been leaders in the Christian movement in

Rome. They had come to Corinth where their skills would probably have been in demand.

They were tent-makers. Now the Greek word that is translated tent-maker in the Bible means someone who works with leather, since tents were made of leather. So it is quite likely that Aquila and his wife could make leather goods of all kinds: tents, awnings to keep the heat off, bags, screens, leather clothing (including armour for the legions – though that was probably in the hands of leather-workers attached to cohorts of soldiers), possibly even sandals (although there was a perfectly good word for cobbler to talk of those who specialized in making footwear).

They had probably rented a workshop in Corinth by the time Paul found them. It was common for members of a particular trade to congregate in the same part of a city. So when Paul arrived in Corinth, needing to work so he would be able to eat and pay his rent, he went to the street where the leather-workers plied their trade. Meeting Aquila and Priscilla, he set up shop with them.

We meet this couple in three places in the New Testament – Corinth, Ephesus, and eventually Rome – which suggests a degree of mobility that was probably not that unusual in the first century. Corinth and Ephesus were bustling towns where demand for leather goods such as tents, awnings, bags, and animal harnesses was pretty high. Corinth, in addition, hosted the biennial Isthmian games, where athletes came from all over the empire to compete, and they and the crowds of spectators drawn to the games would need tents to live in and awnings to shelter under in the heat of the day.

Aquila and Priscilla seemed able to travel, indicating that they were not poor; and wherever they ended up they seemed to host a gathering of believers. When Paul wrote to the Corinthian churches during a stay in Ephesus, Aquila and Priscilla were there, hosting a church in their home (1 Corinthians 16:19) and by the time Paul wrote to the churches in Rome, they were back in that city, hosting a different group of believers in their home (Romans 16:3–5). It suggests a couple with sufficient means to rent accommodation big enough to enable them to offer hospitality to a small gathering of believers.

A shipping magnate

Sea trade was vital to the empire and it is clear from the number of wrecks in the Mediterranean that have been dated to the first century that it was also booming. Ships criss-crossed the ocean between North Africa, Greece, and Rome carrying cargoes of all kinds – in particular, grain and other foodstuffs to the capital itself.

Many people earned a good living from this trade through owning ships, financing voyages, or managing shipments of goods from one country to another. People with the cash came together in consortia to fund specific voyages, bringing essential and luxury goods to Rome from the far-flung corners of the empire and then sharing the profits from the trip. Of course, they shared the risks too since they would lose everything if the ship sank or fell into the hands of pirates. For this reason, the profits from financing sea traffic were substantial.

It would have required a fleet of 1,700 ships to carry Rome's annual demand for grain, olive oil, and wine. Other trade would have doubled the number of ships at sea through the spring to autumn sailing season. This required a large number of shipowners, not to mention the thousands of sailors needed to sail them – even allowing for the use of slaves in the larger galleys.

One of the important staging posts in this trade was Corinth, whose two harbours – Lechaeum on the Adriatic and Cenchrea on the Aegean – and position on the main east–west trade route through the empire made it a commercial hub.

Phoebe from Cenchrea, Corinth's port city, could well have been involved in this business. The fact that she came to Rome to deliver – and probably explain – Paul's letter suggests that she was free to travel. Her base in Cenchrea where she was host of the church there suggests a maritime source to what wealth she had. Again, she would not have been a member of the super-rich of the empire, but the fact that Paul describes her as a patron to many, including himself, suggests that she had substantial surplus income and was probably of higher rank than Paul (chapter 5 will explore what this means).

Have tools, will travel

And then there was Paul. We tend to think of him as a religious professional, a full-time minister of religion like a modern-day priest or missionary; but this was not so. Like his friends Aquila and Priscilla, he was a tent-maker or leather-worker. And like them, if he did not work, he did not eat.

According to Acts, he worked in Corinth and Thessalonica and we have no reason to doubt that this was his custom: so wherever he travelled, he found a place in a workshop and lived by making goods.

But it was slightly unusual for someone in Paul's position to live this way. He could have earned his living by receiving support from the churches that he had established in various cities across the empire. He says as much in 1 Corinthians 9 before stressing that he has chosen not to. Some travelling philosophers – and that is how Paul would have been seen by many of his contemporaries – lived by receiving the patronage of a rich family in any city they visited.

More importantly, as we saw earlier in the chapter, the social elites looked down on manual labour and so they would have found a new religion being taught by someone engaged in such a trade quite unappealing. Paul was aware of this and some have suggested that he was slightly ashamed of his need to work. But the fact that he chose to make tents, when it is clear from the Corinthian correspondence that there were families in that city at least who were quite prepared to offer him financial support, suggests that he saw manual labour as more than just a means to an end.

Working and eating

Which brings us back to 2 Thessalonians 3:10. For the vast majority of people in the empire, this saying was an obvious truism. It was essential to get a day's work and the money it yielded if one was going to eat. But, as we shall see in chapter 5, Paul is having a none too subtle dig at a way of living that involved being the client of a rich benefactor. His ideal was that everyone who could work did work so that they in turn could be benefactors of those in genuine need. And that is why he uses his life of hard manual work as an example for those in his churches to follow.

The life of a slave

It is difficult to be certain of the exact number of slaves in the Roman empire at the time when the Christian church was being born. The best estimate is that there were probably between 10 and 12 million slaves out of a total population of 60 million, or between 16 and 20 per cent of the whole. It means that one in every five or six people you would meet would be a slave.

Of course, the slave population was not evenly spread across the empire. It was quite low in Egypt but in Rome the enslaved probably accounted for a third of residents, 350,000 out of about a million.

It goes without saying that the lot of the slave was not a happy one. They were the possessions of their owners, treated as one tool among many. Indeed the Roman writer Varro in his treatise on agriculture referred to ploughs as "dumb tools" and slaves as "articulate tools".

Generally speaking, life for slaves in the countryside was considerably grimmer than that faced by their urban counterparts. They were worked relentlessly, often chained together and kept at night in blocks no better than prison cells, often in manacles. Many of these slaves were captives of Rome's frequent wars of conquest or runaway urban slaves being punished by their masters. Few slaves were born in the countryside because males and females had little contact.

In the cities the lives of slaves varied depending on the household they were in and the level of skills they had. Slaves with good literacy levels could be put to work as teachers, clerks, or accountants, doing responsible work on behalf of their masters. Much imperial administration was in the hands of slaves. Hundreds of them would work in a variety of clerical functions in households across Rome and in the many Roman colonies strewn through the empire.

Athens

By the first century Athens was a city past its prime. It had been the centre of a major empire. Now it was decaying. Its population had shrunk to around 75,000 and, because it had sided with the wrong people in the civil war that saw Augustus come to power, it had become something of a political backwater.

But it was still seen as the centre of refined culture. Elite Romans learned to speak Greek as children – often from a Greek-speaking nanny. And they aspired to Greek ways, visiting Athens on the empire's equivalent of the European grand tour to soak up Homer and Plato, Aristotle and the classical dramas.

Alexander's empire had brought Greek culture and language to a large part of the world that was now ruled by Rome. It is the reason that the early Christians wrote in Greek. That was the language that most citizens at the eastern end of the empire worked with every day in the school and market-place, the law courts and corridors of power.

And Athens was still a centre of learning. It was a university town with schools of philosophy and rhetoric attracting students and people searching for answers to life's deep problems. It was also a city full of gods. At the height of its power Athens had been where decisions were made about who and what Greek people could officially worship. They even had a council responsible for vetting the claims of gods. It was known as the Areopagus and we encounter it in Acts 17 when the apostle Paul is invited to make his case before it.

By the time Paul arrived in Athens around AD 50, a number of new gods had arrived in the city, clinging to the togas of its new Roman masters. The imperial cult, the fastest growing religion of the period, had taken such a hold that it had amended the architecture of some key city buildings. In particular the portico of Zeus – the head of the Greek pantheon of gods – had been redesigned to accommodate a shrine to the imperial family and the goddess Roma.

The Areopagus stood on Mars Hill opposite the famous city landmarks of the Parthenon and the Acropolis. In its heyday, it was a powerful gathering. It was before the Areopagus that the philosopher Socrates was brought to account for why he was trying to introduce foreign gods into the city. In those days the body had the power of life and death.

Acts 17:16–34 tells us that Paul was invited to speak before it because certain philosophers who had heard him speaking in the market-place thought that he was trying to introduce foreign deities to the city. If that was the case, he needed permission from the Areopagus.

In fact, Paul told his audience, he was not introducing foreign gods at all. Rather, he was bringing into focus a god they had worshipped for years but whose name they had never known. He spoke of seeing an altar to an unknown god – perhaps a statue that had been restored and the name of the deity in whose honour it was originally erected had been lost – and he told his audience that this god had made himself known in his messenger, Jesus, who had been raised from the dead and would one day judge the world.

It is almost certain that the households of Aristobulus and Narcissus mentioned in Romans 16:10–11 were two such places. Both had been taken into the imperial household upon the death of their respective masters. It is clear from what Paul writes that within both of them were followers of Jesus, slaves working in the imperial administration in various capacities.

Buying their freedom

People were forced into slavery for all kinds of reasons and most wanted to gain their freedom as quickly as possible. And the Roman slave system was very porous. It was possible for hard-working and obedient slaves to gain their freedom after a period of time.

One way they did this was to save up their allowance, known as a *peculium*, until they had the price their master had paid for them or could get in the open market if selling them on. The *peculium* came to the slave entirely on the whim of his or her master (though it was usually only given to men). It might have been a tiny percentage of the value of goods the slave had helped to make or market; or it might have been a small payment for the services rendered by the slave to those outside the household – for example, tuition fees if the household ran an education service of some kind.

The Workplace as Church

The workplace was the natural base for mission to take place. The church at Thessalonica appears to be a good example of this. It was a single congregation and does not seem to have met in a home. Indeed there is good evidence that it functioned like a voluntary association (see chapter 5) and was based in the believers' place of work where some of them will also have lived.

The evidence for this lies in what Paul writes to this young group in the two letters he sent in the space of a month or six weeks in either AD 52 or 53, very soon after he had moved on from founding their church.

Acts tells us Paul had stayed with Jason (17:5b), who was probably in the same trade as Paul. As he worked in Jason's workshop, Paul spoke to workers and their customers. And as he spoke, some of these new colleagues believed. Paul talked of being in the workshop "night and day" (1 Thessalonians 2:9), presumably because they ate and slept where they worked. So there would have been plenty of opportunity for the kind of interaction that would have enabled Paul to talk about the Christian faith.

Assuming Paul founded the church this way, it accounts for his description of himself as like a father (2:11), suggesting that these masterless men were formed into an impromptu "family" by Paul and his team.

When Paul moved on, the believers he left behind formed themselves into a workplace voluntary association, with leadership chosen from among themselves. This was Paul's normal practice. The only reference in 1 Thessalonians to leadership of any kind in the nascent Christian community is pretty vague and fluid (5:12–14).

From our point of view, the interesting thing is that Paul describes this group as a church. It appears that for Paul church happened wherever and whenever a group of Christians met together for mutual support and nurture in their Christian faith.

One interesting question it raises is: when did this group gather as church? Perhaps they met on the first day of the week, but there is precious little evidence for this. A single reference in Acts (20:7) says they met on a Sunday but we cannot be certain this was the normal, regular practice (see also 1 Corinthians 16:2, though this does not imply a meeting, only a solo act).

After all, as already noted, no one had a day off, so Sunday was just a normal working day. Day labourers – earning a denarius a shift – had to work every day they could. So it seems likely that the church met when it could: probably either early in the morning or late in the evening – before or after the working day – and over a meal. Certainly Paul seems to have had no sense that one day was more important than another, telling the Colossians not to believe anyone who said otherwise (Colossians 2:16–17). When they met, they'd have shared a meal and learned more about their new faith (see chapter 6 for more in-depth study of Christian gatherings).

For Paul the key thing about the workplace was the opportunity it afforded him to meet people with whom he could share the gospel. We shall see later that homes were crucial for the growth of the early church. But the workplace was too. Indeed in Thessalonica it could well be that the workplace was also the home where they met.

It was through his work that Paul met people. Customers would have come to place orders for his tents; he could well have visited homes where orders had come from in order to measure for a bespoke awning or deliver the finished goods. We can imagine conversations developing over the work-bench that resulted in an invitation to come and eat with the family buying the goods from him. Very soon customers were becoming Christians and small churches were forming in the streets around his workshop.

Charge it to My Account

If a slave ran away, their owner would often put up a sign asking for them to be returned, much as modern people may put up signs when an animal goes missing. If found, the slave would be punished for theft because in running away they had robbed the owner of the value of their labour.

This might throw light on Paul's remark to the slave owner Philemon in a letter he wrote to him in the late 50s AD concerning his slave called Onesimus. Paul says to his friend that if Onesimus owes him anything he should charge it to Paul's account (Philemon 18). This is quite a bold offer on Paul's part because many days' worth of labour would amount to a large number of denarii (a denarius being the usual rate for a day labourer).

➡   Of course, Paul does not expect Philemon to collect the debt. Rather it seems that he is gently pointing out that Onesimus has become a Christian and is therefore now a "brother" of Philemon, so he should consider offering his slave not punishment but freedom. This is a bold request and it goes against Roman practice and could even be technically illegal.

But Paul makes it, and tradition has it that Philemon acceded to his request because Onesimus became a leader in the church later in the first century and one of the first people to make a collection of Paul's letters for safe-keeping. If this is true, he really did live up to his name, which means "useful".

It is possible that Onesimus has not run away at all but rather has been sent by Philemon to offer Paul assistance while he is in prison. So useful has he proved to Paul and so confident is Paul that he is about to be released, that he asks Philemon to release Onesimus from slavery so that he can become a member of Paul's travelling team.

On this understanding Philemon 18 becomes a request that Philemon should allow Onesimus access to any of the *peculium* that has accrued to him. Wrongdoing here would then be a vague reference to Onesimus having stayed away from Philemon for longer than anticipated – this is Paul's fault as much as it is the slave's, he implies.

Whatever the precise context for the letter, it is clear that Paul's overwhelming desire is that Philemon release Onesimus from slavery and accept him as a brother in Christ.

The payment served as an incentive to the slave to behave well and work hard. It was, in a sense, a productivity bonus. Slaves in receipt of it were more likely to knuckle down to their job, not to cause any trouble and hence to maximize their value to their owner.

And it helped allay the fears that the elite had that they would all be murdered in their beds by rebellious slaves. There were huge numbers of them compared to the wealthy rulers of the cities and they all knew the stories of the slave Spartacus, who had led a revolt against Rome. A little payment, so the thinking went, meant that slaves would work for their freedom rather than rebel to seize it.

But punishments for disobedience or incompetence, laziness or running away were harsh. Slaves could be killed on the spot for relatively mild misdemeanours such as dropping the glassware at a dinner party. They could be banished to the country estates of their owners where their treatment would be harsh.

Many of the elite had huge numbers of slaves. Pliny the Younger, a governor in Pontus and Bithynia in the early second century, had 4,116 slaves working on his estates and in his villas in town. He was not unusual in that, except that he had a reputation for treating his slaves pretty well overall.

CHAPTER 4

BREAD AND CIRCUSES

When they were not working, the people of the empire's cities were eating or playing, or both. Often they would do this in the company of others in groups known as *collegia,* or voluntary associations that brought together people of the same trade or philosophical bent. Much of this activity had a religious flavour and it took place in a temple or was focused on the eating of food offered to a god and eaten in his name.

The daily diet of the majority was pretty basic and poor – grains, gruel, water, and cheap wine, supplemented on occasion by vegetables, fish, and very rarely meat. But occasionally *collegia* would offer them a genuine banquet and through the year they were able to feast on a range of entertainments, many of them laid on free by the wealthier inhabitants of their city.

The elite ate some eye-popping dishes: stuffed dormice were a favourite, as was a lamb's womb stuffed with minced and spiced meat; some even served the teats from a sow's udder (pig being a hugely popular meat across the empire except in Judea). But even in the homes of the rich, everyday food was pretty run-of-the-mill.

Our daily bread

For breakfast most Romans just had bread. The very poorest would have had a gruel made from cheap grains or lentils (a little like the dhal served in many Asian countries today). Even the wealthier households did not set great store by breakfast; most would have had bread, nuts, and possibly a little cheese.

Lunch too was a light meal in the homes of the wealthy, as they tended to eat a main meal that could start in the late afternoon and last into the evening. For many craft-workers and others who had to work through the day to earn enough to eat at all, lunch was more than likely what was left uneaten from breakfast and eaten on the run; a lot would have had nothing at all.

For poor and middling sort of people, food prepared and eaten at home would have been cold. Most who lived in *insulae* or above their workshops did not have the means to cook anything at home. So bread and cheese, pastries, nuts, and dried fruit, as well as raw vegetables, could be readied and consumed at home. But hot food – most likely a stew of vegetables and lentils or grains, perhaps a fish stew – would have to be bought at a local tavern or café and either eaten there or brought home to be shared with the family. This would have been cheaper than buying fuel for a stove or brazier and a lot less risky.

Conversations over food and wine

There is no need to read far into the New Testament to encounter meal times. Jesus is frequently pictured eating with friend and foe alike, and summary statements about life in the early church often include reference to breaking bread and eating in one another's homes.

Eating in groups was common throughout the cities of the empire. What could be more convivial than gathering after work with friends, chatting about the day and eating and drinking together? And there were a number of ways that people could do it. The most obvious one was that they gathered in the pub at the end of the day. Excavations at Pompeii have unearthed a significant number of places where this probably happened, bars with paintings on the walls that show people drinking, eating, and playing dice.

And, from lists of prices also found, this does not seem to have been an extravagant pastime. Cheap wine could be bought for a quarter of a sestertius (which in turn is a quarter of a denarius, the average day's wage for a labourer), and a plate of basic stew for a similar amount.

It is clear that such bars were places people went to relax at the end of the day, eat and drink, and meet friends. Playing dice, often for small wagers, was clearly also a common activity, judging by the number of times it turns up in wall-paintings.

Associations

But there were more formal ways that people – even quite ordinary working people – met to eat. This was through *collegia* or voluntary associations. We know a lot about these from inscriptions written in stone that have been uncovered all over the empire. They tell us that such groups met in every city and many go into some detail about the rules governing their meetings.

Associations were clubs of people with a common interest. Most of them were either work-related or attached to a particular religious cult. Many ensured that you would get a proper funeral when you died (though these reached the peak of their popularity in the second century). But some seemed to exist for no other reason than providing a group of friends with whom to share a meal. So, in Pompeii there was a club called the Late-Night Drinkers. It was not unique. *Collegia* with similar names appear all over the empire.

A few associations were official in that they had been established with imperial approval to celebrate a significant local deity or even more likely a deified member of the imperial family. But most were informal and were subject to periodic bans by the authorities, who feared that they would get out of hand or become places where treason was plotted. Various imperial edicts outlawing *collegia*, especially those that met in private homes, were passed from the reign of Augustus onwards. But these did not seem to dampen people's enthusiasm for starting them up.

In an exchange of letters between the emperor Trajan and his man in Pontus and Bithynia, Pliny, the latter asks whether he should grant permission for a voluntary association of fire-fighters to be set up in one of the towns under his jurisdiction. After all, Augustus himself had encouraged such societies to form in Rome during his reign. Trajan is unequivocal in his response: such societies, however innocently they start out, he says, always become places of sedition.

The rules of the house

Whenever people got together for a formal meal – whether an association gathering in a temple or club hall or a dinner in a well-off person's *domus* – there were social niceties, even rules, to be followed.

So, an inscription concerning a society formed to honour the goddess Diana and the deified Antonius, in Lanuvium in Italy, outlines that banquets would be called from time to time by a club official called the *magister cenarum* (master of dinners). His role was to ensure there would be adequate wine, bread, and sardines for all the diners attending. He was also responsible for ensuring that the dining-room was properly set up and that waiting staff were on hand to serve the guests. It is unclear whether he was expected to do all this out of his own pocket or whether there was a wealthy patron who picked up the tab for such special feasts. The latter is more likely, unless the *magister* was also the patron of the association.

The inscription goes on to tell us how guests at the dinner were to behave. In particular, as well as a general admonition to "peace and quiet", members were expressly forbidden from discussing business over the meal. That was to be reserved for the business meeting that preceded the feasting.

And there were fines for bad behaviour. If a diner moved from his place on the couch in the triclinium in a way that disturbed those next to him, he would be fined four sesterces. If a guest verbally abused another guest or caused uproar by his actions, he would be fined twelve sesterces. If he insulted a club official, the fine was twenty sesterces. Such hefty amounts would have ensured that people were on their best behaviour.

The wall-paintings from the bars of Pompeii suggest no such decorum was observed, despite the best efforts of the landlord! Pictures show fighting and carousing, with words written beneath them advising patrons that they will be thrown out for brawling or lewd behaviour in public.

A leisurely dinner

Any formal meal, from an association gathering in a temple to an elite dinner party, followed a fairly set pattern. The event would happen in two distinct halves. The first, known as the *deipnon* (Greek for supper), was, as its name suggests, a formal meal eaten by diners reclining in the triclinium. Large banquets might have had diners in several rooms of a *domus* on couches specially brought in for the occasion, or people (especially women and younger members of families) sitting on chairs and benches around the atrium and in the peristyle (assuming the weather was good).

Slaves would serve food off trays, which the reclining guests would eat with their fingers. The Romans had not invented forks. So they would eat soup or stew with a spoon but meat, fish, and vegetables were cut up – either by the servants or by the diners themselves – and eaten with fingers. Other slaves would have been on hand to wash the diners' hands at various points during the meal.

The second part of a formal banquet was known as the symposium. This would have been a time of entertainment or of lively philosophical discussion or possibly a mixture of both. The start of the symposium was usually signalled by the arrival of jugs of wine and water – Romans rarely drank wine undiluted – and the offering of formal toasts to the gods, the household's patron, and the host of the banquet.

If entertainment was the order of the day, the toasting would be followed by the arrival of the flute-girl and a variety of dancers and entertainers. Such symposia would sometimes become little more than orgies, with guests filled with wine availing themselves of women who had been provided by the host of the banquet.

The latest ideas

But symposia were often places where the latest ideas would be discussed and debated. Sometimes the host would have a visiting philosopher or teacher staying who would lead a discussion on some elevated topic.

More often than not, there would also be entertainment at such symposia but it would take the form of recitals by skilled musicians or poetry readings, even the acting of scenes from great dramas.

And at every symposium, it seems, there was singing. Usually, there would be at least a hymn in praise of the deity in whose name the banquet was being held. If there was a flute-girl present, that usually meant a session of communal singing was in the offing. One type of song frequently used took a familiar tune but the host or a selected guest would sing the first line, and then another guest had to sing a witty rejoinder as the second line.

The Roman writer Plutarch did not favour such singing at symposia since it usually meant that things would get out of hand as the men drank more wine and became more raucous. But he recognized that such songs, known as *scolia*, served a solemn purpose, often sung solo to a god and offering a moral for the diners to think about. He even talks about symposia where a lyre would be passed around and any guest who was able would play and sing.

But, for Plutarch, it was the conversation that mattered, because that ensured the guests remained focused and sober. He suggested that a whole range of topics could be selected – from history, philosophy, current events, religious ideas – that would lead to the guests becoming enthusiastic for courageous or kind actions, charity, or humane deeds in society. And such thoughts, he argued, would prevent the guests from getting hopelessly drunk.

Meeting to remember Jesus

It is quite possible that when Paul describes the Corinthians gathering to celebrate the Lord's Supper in 1 Corinthians 11, what he has in mind is a form of symposium. It is likely that Christians across the empire met in all kinds of contexts to eat together and worship while they did so. One of the first independent accounts of the Christian gathering that we have comes from Pliny, who (as quoted earlier) told Trajan in a letter around AD 115:

. . . they met regularly on a fixed day before dawn to sing responsively a hymn to Christ as to a god, and to bind themselves by oath, not to some crime, but not to commit fraud, theft, or adultery, nor to falsify their trust, nor to refuse to return a deposit when called upon to do so. When this was over, it was their custom to depart and to reassemble later to take food – but ordinary, harmless food.

It is clear from this that Christians of all kinds – and this information, as appears elsewhere in this letter, comes from the testimony of two slaves he had tortured to extract evidence – met to eat together, talk about lofty things in the presence of their God, sing a hymn or two, and commit themselves to fellowship with one another. In other words, they held a symposium.

Now, it is almost certain, because we know that most of the first Christians were not rich people (a question explored in chapter 7), that the gatherings of the early church took place in a variety of locations and that their "feasting" would have been pretty basic. But it also seems clear that, whenever they gathered, the model of their meeting was the symposium, something that would have been familiar to them from their upbringing wherever they lived in the empire – even if many of them had rarely, if ever, experienced one.

When he wrote to the Ephesians, Paul probably had in mind the kind of thinking we have just seen in Plutarch. In 5:18–20 he suggests that it is better to be filled with the Holy Spirit than drunk on wine. He clearly thought that Christian teaching, inspired by and leading to an experience of the Holy Spirit, was far better than drinking to excess. What is almost certain is that his first hearers would have picked this up immediately because of their frequent experience of symposia (see the box on p. 85 to see how this applies to 1 Corinthians 11–14).

The great gore-fest

While the symposium might have been an elegant, quiet, refined occasion – assuming all the guests did not get drunk – most Roman entertainment was anything but. The amphitheatres in every major city played host to spectacles that were gory beyond imagining. In 100 days of games at the dedication of the Colosseum in Rome, thousands of men and animals met their death to entertain crowds of 50,000 cheering onlookers.

The entertainments in the arena took a variety of forms: gladiatorial games where professional gladiators, condemned criminals, and slaves fought one another to the death; animal spectaculars where exotic creatures were hunted and killed before an audience; and the throwing of criminals and social deviants (occasionally including Christians) to wild animals.

Although such games had been a feature of city life for a couple of centuries, it is with the beginning of the empire that they took on the form seen in such Hollywood blockbusters as *Ben Hur* and *Gladiator*. All across the empire in the first century, enterprising aristocrats put on spectaculars at their own expense, inviting the populace to come and enjoy the games and the handouts of food that accompanied them.

The numbers involved in the games staged by the emperor in Rome are jaw-dropping. In AD 52 Claudius put on a naval battle on a lake near Rome. The two opposing navies were made up of 19,000 conscripted combatants, kept at their task by members of the palace guard who would bombard the ships of both sides with missiles. In the end the survivors – less than half the starting line-up – were spared death. The 11,000 animals used in a show mounted by Trajan to mark his conquest of modern Romania were not as lucky. That 123-day event also saw 9,138 gladiators fighting to the death and countless criminals fed to wild animals.

The Roman populace was fascinated by exotic animals. So traders and imperial agents trawled the known world looking for lions, tigers, antelopes, elephants, even crocodiles. These were not paraded in zoos but set to work in the empire's amphitheatres hunting or being hunted. Not many lived for long. The spectacle of slaughter reached its zenith under the emperor Commodus – he of *Gladiator* fame – who killed 100 lions and bears in a single morning show.

Aphrodisias

The power of Rome was seen in its legions and control of the seas. But much more it was displayed in spectacular art. Imperial Rome created a myth about itself that gripped people's imagination as they worked, as they were entertained, and especially as they worshipped.

We see this clearly in sites all over the Roman world. But nowhere more clearly than in a temple complex unearthed in the city of Aphrodisias in modern-day Turkey.

The Sebasteion is an impressive suite of buildings that is part worship centre and part imperial soap opera, with stone reliefs telling the story of the rise of the Roman empire using images drawn from Greek and Roman mythology. There are forty-five panels on the north and south sides of a long, narrow courtyard between two temples dedicated to the Greek god Aphrodite and the imperial family (*Sebastaios* is the Greek rendering of Augustus).

There is a relief picturing Claudius subduing the Britons. He is pictured as a Greek hero or god, naked and triumphant, standing over an image of Britannia as a defeated Amazon. In his hand would have been a spear (though it has been lost over the centuries) poised to strike the fatal blow if she does not submit to his rule.

On another, Claudius is pictured, again as a Greek hero, bestriding the sea and land and receiving from earth and ocean gifts that indicate his utter supremacy even over the forces of nature.

Yet another panel shows Nero, again carved as a Greek god, defeating Armenia. And another pictures an emperor flanked by a woman on his right side, probably depicting the senate or people of Rome, who is crowning him, maybe with laurels. To his left, a distraught female figure kneels and looks out of the panel at the viewer. It is an image of the complete dominion of the empire, with the woman seeming to say that any resistance to its claim is useless.

The complex was built by local people, using local sculpture styles and funded by two local elite families. So this was not something forced on an unwilling populace. Rather it was a monument to Rome's ability to persuade at least the upper echelons of society across the empire that it was the only game in town and throwing in their lot with imperial power was the way to prosper. ➡

But the complex was used by ordinary citizens who came to worship their local goddess. Only now, she was pictured in a scene where her fate was linked to that of Aeneas in a way that linked the fates of the cities of Aphrodisias and Rome closely together. (Aeneas is a hero of the Trojans in Homer's *The Iliad* who, in Roman mythology, was seen as a type of the emperor. Virgil made him a hero of his poem *The Aeneid*, written in honour of the rise of Augustus.) Every time they came to the altars here, they were worshipping a local deity and the Roman superpower personified in the imperial family.

Displays of imperial power

The games were an opportunity for the emperors and aristocracy to display their power, so they were occasions where the social pecking order of the empire was very clearly on display for all to see.

The emperor – or in a provincial arena, the leading aristocrat who was putting on the games at his own expense – sat in a gilded box with the best view of the arena. Around him, in special seating, the senators and knights sat, adorned in their togas with various amounts of purple on display. Soldiers had reserved places away from the civilian population. The ordinary Roman citizens were expected to wear their white togas – the equivalent of Sunday best. Married men were separated from bachelors, and they sat apart from boys under sixteen, who were corralled in a separate block with their teachers. Priests and vestal virgins (treated as honorary men because of their special role in the religions of the community) had reserved seating near the front of the arena. Women and the very poor, often dressed in grey (because that was all they had), sat at the top of the tiered seating, furthest from the action.

These spectacles were designed to display the way society was ordered. While everyone enjoyed a free show, no one was in any doubt where they sat in the social pecking order (see chapter 5). And as they watched hundreds of men dying in the arena below them, they were in no doubt of the glue that held the empire together: the absolute power of the ruling order, dominated by the emperor and his legions. Every time the audience witnessed a spectacular staged battle, they were being reminded that Rome was what it was because it was the most ruthless and powerful military machine ever to roll over the face of the earth.

They were also witnessing the Roman judicial order at work. The criminals trooping into the arena to die were being publicly executed for a whole range of crimes. The entertainment held the message that wrongdoing in the empire would be met with lethal force.

First-century celebs

But the crowds did not just flock to the arenas out of fear or because it was free. They went because they loved it. Gladiators were the nearest the Roman world had to celebrities. Paintings of them adorned the walls of public porticos; etchings of them were sold in the markets. There was a whole industry meeting the demand of fans for artefacts lauding their favourite arena warrior – figurines, lamps, statuettes, dinner-plates with fighting gladiators on them; even a baby's feeding bottle found in the ruins of Pompeii was adorned with a gladiator image.

A graffito from Pompeii – where the amphitheatre would regularly stage shows involving gladiator fights and animal hunts – attests how popular the fighting men were: "Celadus, thrice victor and thrice crowned, the young girl's heart-throb." Roman brides reportedly wanted to have their hair parted with a spear that had been dipped in the blood of a defeated, and thus dead, gladiator.

The Roman historian Tacitus summed up the grip that gladiators had on the whole population with his comment: "when you enter the lecture halls what else do you hear the young men talking about?"

A day at the races

The other way to become a sporting celebrity in the empire was to be a charioteer, though to hit the big time you had to come to Rome and compete at the Circus Maximus, where chariot-racing was held. Alexandria in Egypt also had a race-track but elsewhere they were more likely to hold races on wasteland just outside the city on a course marked out for the purpose.

Chariot-racing was a substantial business in Italy and especially Rome, with associations or companies forming to buy the equipment and horses and train slaves or willing freedmen – many charioteers were army veterans – to race. Often whole cities would split into factions, each backing a particular team, with lots of money being gambled on the outcome.

While driving a chariot was hugely skilled, chariot-racing was not all good clean athletic endeavour. Many drivers tried to force their opponents off the track on corners, resulting in gruesome injuries and many deaths at each meeting. But for the winners the potential earnings could be enormous. One successful driver at games put on by the emperor Domitian earned fifteen purses of gold in an hour. And Juvenal reckoned a charioteer at the top of his game could earn a hundred times more than an advocate in the courts. And, of course, building and decorating the chariots, feeding and cleaning up after the horses, and creating the charioteers' costumes all created work for the craft-workers on the city's back streets.

The play's the thing

Of course, you could have an evening out that did not involve watching people hacking each other to death. Every city had a theatre and there was a vibrant theatrical culture on offer.

It was still possible to see a Greek tragedy, though they tended not to be performed in their entirety. Much more popular were bawdy one-act farces, the *atellana* and *mimus*. With their themes of love affairs and adultery, coarse humour and much innuendo, they appealed to the working masses looking for an escape from the drudgery of life.

The leisured classes were much more likely to enjoy the pantomime. This was a form usually full of tragic themes. A choir would sing the story while a single actor/dancer would play a succession of different parts, often involving costume changes, to interpret the words being sung. Often pantomimes, performed by travelling players or trained household slaves, formed the centre-piece of a symposium at an elite family's banquet.

The theatrical profession was generally treated with some disdain: actors and dancers had low social status and were often the slaves of wealthy householders. But there was money to be made from the theatre if the performers were good. So there were some theatrical troupes who toured the cities, putting on shows in theatres and private homes.

Running for your life

Paul's letters are littered with references to athletics and the games of the arena. In one celebrated example in his first letter to the church at Corinth, he speaks of the race in which all runners compete, of athletes exercising self-control so that they might win the prize, a wreath (1 Corinthians 9:24–27).

This is probably not accidental, for Corinth was the site of a major biennial athletics event, the Isthmian games, in which Paul would probably have been involved during his time in the city as a supplier of tents and awnings to competitors and spectators.

Athletics was important throughout the empire but especially in the east, in Greece and Asia Minor. Most successful athletes – many of them army veterans – were professionals, training rigorously, eating a carefully planned diet. But people everywhere extolled the virtues of running and athletic training for a healthy life.

The games consisted of many familiar events. Running events took place over various distances from 200 yards to the marathon. Sometimes races were run in armour and carrying weapons to reinforce the link between the games and military discipline. There were also throwing events – the discus and javelin in particular – and jumping, boxing, wrestling, and a fearsome event known as the *pankration*. While boxing and wrestling had rules, though they were not fought in a ring and lasted until one of the contestants was knocked out or collapsed from exhaustion, the *pankration* was a fight with no holds barred. Only gouging and biting were forbidden. Fights took place in well-watered ground, making them a mud-fest that often ended when one competitor was killed or seriously injured and could not fight on.

As in indoor sports in the gymnasium, competitors – all men – competed naked, and for this reason many conservative elements in the Roman west disapproved, which could explain why athletics was slow to catch on in these parts of the empire, including Rome. But games were held by Caligula in AD 37 and 39, Claudius in AD 44, and Nero in AD 60. It was not until Domitian's reign in the 80s that regular games were instituted.

A rich source of metaphors

While the games provide an obvious back-drop to 1 Corinthians 9, there are references to them in most of Paul's letters. Words such as "strive", "conflict", "spectacle", and "prize" all owe their origins to the arena.

One of the most startling metaphors Paul uses from the arena is in 1 Corinthians, where he talks about having fought wild beasts in Ephesus (1 Corinthians 15:32). There is no way that he could ever have fought such beasts in reality, as he would not have survived the experience! But it is a rich and compelling picture of competing against those who were attacking his ministry as he travelled the world.

A message of peace

It is also possible that the blood, horror, and violence of the arena gave rise to a somewhat callous and brutalized popular culture across the empire. Life was cheap and force was met with force. Punishments were brutal and swift, and people tended to look out only for their own interests, often meeting a rival's barbs with fist or blade.

It is noteworthy that the early Christian message does not play down the gory event upon which it is based – namely the cross of Jesus. Crucifixion was a particularly brutal and protracted form of execution that the Romans used to reinforce their claims to absolute power. Paul stresses that the cross lies at the heart of the faith, often playing up the stark reality of the cross in the way he describes it. For instance, in 1 Corinthians 1:18 – 2:5 he uses the phrase "Christ, the crucified one" twice to emphasize that the power and wisdom of God are found not in the lecture halls of the sophisticated but in the shattered body of his Son.

But Christians were not to be people of violence. Everywhere the New Testament talks about how to face opposition, the emphasis is on being gentle, on seeking peace, and on overcoming evil with good. Power for the Christians was to be found as it was for Christ in the way of suffering.

Food, famine, and philanthropy

Food was a constant problem in the ancient world. Many lived at or below subsistence, meaning that they needed to work each day in order to buy what food they could to keep body and soul together. Food production was susceptible to interruption because of bad weather, conflict, or inept farming practice. Absolute famine was rare, but shortages and high prices were all too common.

The food supply across the Roman empire was precarious. Millions of tons of grain had to be shipped to Rome from Egypt – the imperial bread-basket – to keep its growing population fed. All cities were similarly dependent on imports, as local agriculture could not support all the demands of growing urban centres.

There is abundant evidence of Corinth – and the whole region – being beset with food shortages all through the AD 50s. Three times during this decade the office of curator of the grain supply (*curator annonae*) was held by a man called Dinippus. This office was only required when there was a problem with the supply of grain to the city. It was a highly prestigious office, possibly equal to the president of the games, the official tasked with organizing the biennial Isthmian games near Corinth.

Like all offices in the Roman empire, this one was held by a man of considerable wealth because his role was to use his resources to manage – even manipulate – the market in grain so that even the poorest could continue to afford to buy it or the bread made from it. In short, he bought grain at whatever price he could find it and sold it at whatever price the leading citizens thought the city could bear. No wonder inscriptions testify to his wonderful benefaction of the city over many years.

Such officials had existed in Rome itself since early in Augustus's reign. Indeed as he consolidated his hold on power, he took care of the grain supply – ensuring that the ordinary people of the capital knew from whose hand their daily bread was coming. From AD 6 a permanent post of *praefectus annonae* (prefecture of the grain supply) was established and held by a man from the equestrian class (just below senatorial rank, and of considerable wealth and status; see chapter 5).

Keeping the masses happy

One of the *praefectus's* roles was to ensure that the ones entitled to it received a regular allocation of grain. Not everyone received this largesse. The very poor, for instance, who you might think needed it more than anyone, did not receive it. The very poor did not "vote". The respectable plebs, however, did have a say in how popular the government was and well-fed plebs tended to vote for the *status quo*. So, on production of a ticket, they received their grain dole.

The effects of food shortages were all too predictable – hence the desire on the part of those in authority to ensure the populace was well fed. A second-century Ephesian inscription notes: "thus it happens at times that the populace is plunged into disorder and riots". And the Roman historian Seneca says of Rome in AD 40–41: "We were threatened with the worst evil that can befall men during a siege – the lack of provisions." In the eastern city of Aspendus during the reign of Tiberius, a mob was narrowly averted from lynching the local magistrate because he was able to persuade them that certain speculators were responsible for the food shortages that had afflicted the population. They left him alone to go and sack the speculators' estates instead!

When grain supplies got tight in first-century Galatia, the governor ordered all the inhabitants of Pisidian Antioch to declare how much grain they held, stressing that hoarding would be severely punished and ruling that the price would not be allowed to exceed one denarius per *modius*. It is possible that this draconian measure forms the back-drop to John's vision in Revelation where he hears a voice saying, "A quart of wheat for a day's pay" (Revelation 6:6).

Crisis? What crisis?

It could well be that such food shortages formed the back-drop to Paul's eye-catching phrase in 1 Corinthians 7:26: "in view of the impending crisis". He does not elaborate but the context – whether it is wise to add to the population or get married – suggests that he is offering pastoral advice to a community facing very real economic hardship.

Part of Paul's response is that famines and such things might presage the end of the world – certainly some Christians thought that was the case. But Paul is also immensely practical. In chapter 7, he suggests that refraining from sex to avoid conceiving more children is not advisable. He observes that marriages can go ahead if the couple cannot wait but that they might want to think about the practicalities of it before they do.

And it is very likely that he has the same issue in mind later when, talking about what happens when the believers come together for their communal meal and to celebrate holy communion, he says that people who have should share with those who lack.

In 1 Corinthians 11:17–34 two groups of believers are contrasted. One has food and drink aplenty – certainly enough drink to be drunk by sunset (the time when the working poor would turn up for the meal). The other has nothing. They are unable to bring any food to the communal meal. Paul's advice is that the "haves" wait for the "have nots" to arrive, the implication being that when they do, what food there is will be shared among all the guests (though Paul does not spell that out, perhaps because he might have felt it inappropriate to do so in a letter and this is what he intended to talk about at greater length when he arrived soon [11:34]).

Somewhere to pull up a chair

The early Christians gathered in homes across the empire. There were no purpose-built churches for the first 250 years of the movement's life. So in Corinth, a few believers – maybe twenty-five or thirty – would gather in various homes around the city. It is likely that Chloe (1 Corinthians 1:11) and Stephanas (16:15–17) and Aquila and Priscilla, before they moved, each hosted a gathering.

There is some debate, however, about where the congregations gathered. Some historians argue that there were sufficient people of means in the Corinthian churches to have *domus*-style homes with plenty of space to host a group of two or three dozen. Others suggest that most of the Corinthian believers would have been craft-workers – like Aquila and Priscilla – who would have lived in *insulae* or possibly rooms behind or above their rented workshops.

There is no reason why we cannot imagine the believers gathering in a variety of locations and housing types in the city. We know from Romans 16:23 that Gaius had a home in Corinth and played host to everyone from the churches around the city. But the fleeting reference does not allow certainty as to whether he took the whole group at one time or whether he was a hospitable man who invited believers to meals regularly but only in quite small numbers.

Planned menu or pot-luck?

A second question arises when we think about these gatherings. Were the meals hosted by a householder who provided all the food for the

A Christian Symposium?

Some of the most difficult material in Paul's first letter to the church at Corinth comes in chapters 11–14. It tackles issues such as women at worship, how people should behave at the communal meals, and the whole area of something called spiritual gifts. On that last subject he observes that it would better if the neighbours passing through your meeting did not think you were out of your minds (1 Corinthians 14:23)!

Making sense of it becomes a whole lot easier when we realize that Paul is talking about what happens when a small group of believers comes together for a meal and a time of teaching and learning. Everything that Paul talks about in this section takes place in the context of a meal.

So, is this a symposium? It looks very likely that the early Christians used the symposium as a model for their gatherings. It would have been the obvious thing to do for two reasons.

The first is that when people got together for a banquet of any kind – whether a dinner party with neighbours at home or a formal dinner at a voluntary association – it invariably took the form of a symposium. That is to say that a dinner was followed by a period of structured conversation and/or entertainment. If the symposium took the form of a conversation, then it was usually introduced by the host or an invited guest speaker, before being thrown open for everyone to join in.

The second is that when the early Christians gathered they seemed always to remember Jesus by sharing bread and wine together, the key elements of the Last Supper as recorded in the gospels (see, for example, Mark 14:12–26, an event which itself has all the appearance of a symposium).

gathering or were they pot-luck suppers where all the diners brought food with them to share?

One thing we can be fairly certain about is that when the believers met they shared a meal. The Lord's Supper that Paul speaks of in 1 Corinthians 11 was not just a tiny piece of bread and a sip of wine, as it is in most churches these days. It was a meal, during which someone reminded the diners that Jesus had eaten bread and wine with his friends and told them to do the same in memory of him every time they ate, because the bread symbolized his body and the wine his blood.

The economic circumstances of the early Christians considered in this chapter suggest that some would have been fairly poor and possibly not able to bring anything to share, while others had the wherewithal to buy two loaves of bread on the day the Christians assembled for their symposium.

It is suggested in 1 Corinthians 11:20–22 that some were arriving at the supper with nothing and that those with plenty were not sharing as Paul had instructed them to. The wording here strongly suggests a pot-luck supper rather than a dinner where the host provides all the food.

Chapter 5 will look at the gatherings in more detail.

CHAPTER 5

A PLACE IN THE WORLD

People in the Roman empire knew their place. They knew where they fitted in the social hierarchy and it mattered that they not only maintained that place but improved it through hard work and making good connections with those higher up the pecking order.

But though the broad outlines of the social hierarchy can be mapped fairly clearly, the degrees of difference both within and between social groups make the world of Roman cities fascinating in its subtlety and complexity.

Dividing lines

Social status in the Roman world depended on a number of factors. The basic distinction between people was simple: are you a slave or a free person? Between 16 and 20 per cent of the empire's population were slaves – though in Italy and Rome itself, this rose to a third. These people had no rights – they were unable to own property, unable legally to marry, and so unable to have legitimate children; in short, they were the property of their masters.

Free people, a majority of the empire, fell into two camps – Roman citizens and others, the latter (known as *peregrini*) outnumbering the former (except in Rome) by around ten to one. In Rome most people were citizens but in the provinces only the local elites and a few others were granted the privilege.

The exception to this general rule was the string of Roman colonies established across the empire. Cities such as Philippi, Corinth, and Pisidian Antioch mentioned in the New Testament were either founded or revived by an expansionist Rome, looking to extend its influence, protect its trade routes, and find places to settle veterans of the legions.

Colonies, wherever they were, were treated as though they were suburbs of Rome with Roman law being enforced and a Roman style of government in operation. It meant that significant numbers of the population, maybe up to a third, were citizens.

And then there was a distinction between patrician and plebeian. At issue here was the distinction between those with long-standing claims to Roman citizenship, and the wealth and power that supported them, and everyone else. The former group made up the senatorial, equestrian, and decurial orders, while the latter group comprised the bulk of ordinary people struggling to get by (see pp. 90–91).

Everyone in their place

At the top of the pecking order of privilege were two groups who made up the administrative aristocracy. The first was the senatorial class, limited by Augustus to around 600 people, elected to it by other senators on the basis of their birth, breeding, and wealth. Senators had to have assets – mainly land and property – worth 1,200,000 sesterces or more, roughly 1,200 times the average income of a day labourer.

As their title suggests, they were part of the body that met in the senate in Rome to govern the city and its empire. The senate met fortnightly and was responsible for debating and legislating on a variety of issues such as inheritance and public order, the building of roads, and other public works. But the real power in the land lay in the hands of the imperial household.

The other aristocratic group was the equestrian class – so called because those belonging to it were entitled to a horse from public funds. They were also extremely wealthy, needing assets of 400,000 sesterces. Because their numbers were not limited, aspiring rich provincials and freedmen across the empire could join this class – if invited by a social superior and if they had proved themselves in the army or local administration.

Senators were allowed to wear a broad purple stripe on their togas, while equestrians were allowed a narrow purple band and a gold finger ring. What you wore in the Roman empire was determined by your status.

There was a third group of powerful people in the social pecking order. Known as decurions, they were the provincial urban elite, the men who ran the town councils in Pompeii and Corinth, Ephesus and Alexandria. These were people from a variety of backgrounds. Some were local landowners whose families had always run things and who were now drawn into the administration of imperial affairs locally. Others were wealthy and well-connected men from families aspiring to equestrian rank who were cutting their teeth in the provinces in the hope of gaining preferment.

Their wealth meant that they enjoyed high status and their position gave them privileges, such as eating at public expense on special civic occasions. But like elites everywhere, they were expected to use their wealth to enhance their cities by funding public buildings and organizing games and spectaculars – this was often part of a programme of Romanization in the provinces, to which the decurions were key.

An imperial career ladder

By the first century, as government was growing to keep pace with the expanding empire, what looks like a senatorial and sometimes an equestrian career path began to emerge. The *cursus honorum* was a sequence of government offices that would lead a young man to high office, possibly even elevation to the senate. Often referred to as the magistracy, this series of offices ensured the smooth administration of the empire at all levels and in all places.

Readers of the New Testament come across various Roman magistrates fulfilling functions on various rungs of this ladder. In Acts 18 there is the proconsul Gallio, a significant figure who is rising up the imperial chain of command. In Romans 16:23 there is Erastus, Corinth's city treasurer, a man on a lower rung than Gallio, who might have been an imperial slave or freedman but was someone with some clout in provincial government. And in the gospels, of course, there is Pontius Pilate, a man of equestrian rank, who was the Roman procurator of Judea.

Looking for a hand up

Every citizen who was not a patrician was a plebeian. But even here there was a pecking order. In Rome, the grain dole was only granted to "official" plebs (some 200,000 in the reign of Augustus). These middle-order people had their social status enhanced by being on the list of recipients, but most still had to work as labourers to make ends meet.

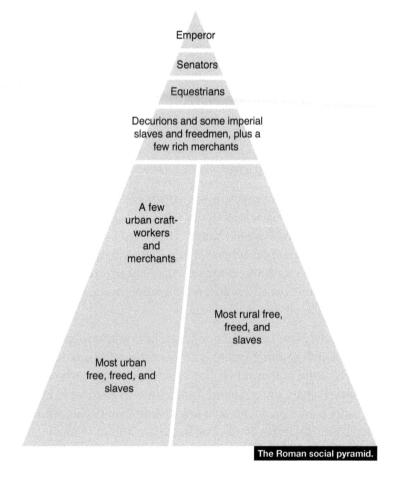

The Roman social pyramid.

Most people were linked to other people through complex webs of patronage and clientage. Slaves were owned by their masters but even freed slaves were still bound by law to their old masters and free people of lower status voluntarily attached themselves to richer, higher-status people in the hope of getting on in the world.

At its simplest this can look like an ordinary commercial transaction. For example, an elite family always buy their bread from a family of bakers nearby. But the men of the baking family will always turn out to support the elite family's men when they are involved in chariot-racing or making a speech in the local forum. Trade buys loyalty and loyalty ensures continued trade.

Such relationships of dependency were everywhere in Roman life. The emperor was at the top of this pyramid of patronage. Without his support even the most able, ambitious, and well-connected senator could not hold high office. But the emperor needed such clients to ensure the smooth running of the empire. And those senators were patrons to their colleagues who were not as well connected.

And so such relationships cascaded down the social pecking order, everyone looking to someone in a slightly better position than they were to give them the nod. And in this way, even those at the bottom of the heap could gain a bit of access to those with power and authority. Clients would look to their patron for practical, financial, or sometimes legal support. And in return the patron was looking for respect, favours, and a pool of followers who could be relied on to turn out when it mattered.

And, of course, it was in no one's interest to upset the applecart. Few questioned the justice of this social hierarchy, for to do so would have harmed both their and their family's prospects of preferment.

It's all about looking the part

This system of patronage underlay a key facet of Roman society that had to do with gaining or losing honour.

Gallio

L. Junius Gallio was proconsul of Achaea between July 51 and June 52. He has a key walk-on role in the New Testament, appearing in Luke's account of Paul's time in Corinth (Acts 18:12–17) and so providing a vital fixed point in New Testament chronology.

Gallio was born L. Annaeus Novatus, son of Seneca the Elder and brother of the famous stoic philosopher Seneca the Younger, but he was adopted by Seneca the Elder's great friend, a leading senator, L. Junius Gallio. He changed his name to L. Junius Gallio Annaeus. With his new sponsor, he seems to have risen through the ranks of imperial service fairly quickly and to have made some powerful friends.

It is an inscription from the city of Delphi that gives us key information about Gallio's career. The inscription is a letter from the emperor Claudius to the city fathers, written when Gallio was in office in the region. Claudius describes his official as "my friend and proconsul", indicating that Gallio was indeed blessed with friends in high places.

The reason the inscription is so important is that it gives us a very precise date for Gallio's term of office. It begins with the words: "Tiberius Claudius Caesar Augustus Germanicus, 12th year of tribunician power, acclaimed emperor for the 26th time, father of the fatherland, sends greetings . . ." It means the letter was sent in the spring of AD 52 and, since Gallio was already proconsul and the one-year term of office ran from July to June, he almost certainly held the post from July 51 to June 52.

As with many men who rubbed shoulders with the most powerful in the empire, his life was somewhat precarious. He survived the death of Claudius, almost certainly at the hands of his successor, Nero, in AD 54 and continued to hold senior posts in Nero's administration.

But he could not survive the reign of the maniacal Nero. Gallio's brother, called Seneca after his father, plotted against Nero in AD 65 and committed suicide rather than face trial before the senate. And Tacitus in his *Annals* tells us that in the febrile atmosphere following the plot, Gallio feared for his life and eventually seems to have died at his own hand in AD 66 or 67.

His appearance as proconsul in Corinth, however, allows us to date Paul's travels with some accuracy. We know that the tent-making missionary stayed in Corinth for eighteen months (Acts 18:11). It is reasonable to suppose that members of the synagogue who had found his presence and teaching irksome chose the occasion of the arrival of a new proconsul as their moment to bring charges against Paul.

This suggests that the events of Acts 18:12–17 happened in the summer of AD 51. Because Paul received such a favourable outcome in the case, it is likely that he stayed for the rest of Gallio's tenure, deciding to leave in the summer or early autumn of AD 52 when a new proconsul, possibly not so indifferent to the charges brought by his Jewish opponents, was in post.

This means that if Paul stayed eighteen months in Corinth, he probably arrived in the autumn of AD 50. And this fits with another detail that Luke gives us, namely that on arrival in Corinth, Paul met Priscilla and Aquila, who had recently come from Rome because Claudius had expelled the Jews from that city (Acts 18:1).

In the Roman world, honour was not a secondary value – less important than wealth or happiness, for example. It was pivotal and primary. It was also entirely dependent on the opinion of those in the social group to which an individual and their family belonged.

Honour was the value that an individual felt they had in their community, among their peers. It was a claim that the individual in question had social worth that was agreed and acknowledged by others of their class. *Shame* was when honour was taken away from an individual or their family by their peer group because of behaviour deemed to be unworthy.

So honour was much more highly valued than truth or wealth among the elites of the Roman world. Indeed wealth was really only a vehicle to be used to acquire public honour, something much more highly prized than cash in the bank. So someone who hoarded their wealth was dishonourable, whereas someone who lavished it on splendid edifices, such as temples, pavements, and public baths, received great honour as a public benefactor. Honour was simply the public recognition of one's social standing.

People obtained honour in the Roman world in one of two ways. They were either born with it or it was conferred on them because of some act on their part. Scholars refer to these two ways of receiving honour as ascribed and acquired.

Ascribed honour came directly from the family one was born into, not from personal achievement. Senators had honour because they were born with it. This explains why there was such a focus throughout ancient literature on genealogies and extended descriptions of ancestral relations. It also goes a long way to explain why the senate in the first century was constantly debating the dilution of Roman blood by the elevation of so many *nouveaux riches* to the senatorial ranks.

Acquired honour, on the other hand, came through competing for place and position in society. Every social contact that happened outside an individual's family or close circle of friends was a challenge to their honour, an opportunity to acquire more of it, or, of course, the chance to lose it by behaving or performing badly in public.

For example, while insults and lawsuits were obviously a challenge to one's honour, positive everyday occurrences – such as giving a gift, accepting a dinner invitation, debating in the public arena, giving material assistance to the poor, bartering for goods in the market-place, or arranging a marriage – also provided ample opportunity for enhancing or losing one's honour.

It means that, in the Roman world, recognition by and approval from one's social peers was key to one's place in the social pecking order. The group was more important than the individual.

Reading the seating plan

A savvy politician and social observer, Pliny the Younger, wrote to a friend about a banquet he had recently attended where the host had not given equal shares to each of the diners:

The best dishes were set in front of himself and a select few, and cheap scraps of food before the rest of the company. He had even put the wine into tiny little flasks and divided it into three categories, not with the idea of giving his guests the opportunity of choosing, but to make it impossible for them to refuse what was given. One lot was intended for himself and for us, another for his lesser friends (all his friends are graded), and the third for his and our freedmen.

Pliny makes it clear that he disapproved of such hospitality. But it was very common. Even the couches in the triclinium were graded, with the best places given to those who were deemed to have the most honour of those on the guest list.

Pliny tells his friend that he believes in equality at the dining-table, though makes it clear that this means if there are lower-status people at his table, the menu is designed for them and everyone shares it, a kind of lowest common denominator catering policy.

Everywhere one went in public was an opportunity to show off one's status. The seats in the amphitheatres were graded according to social rank and certain types of clothing were restricted to certain orders of people. We have seen that purple stripes of different widths marked out senators and equestrians, but the toga itself marked out citizens from non-citizens – only the former were allowed to wear it. And Augustus used legislation to ensure that the toga – and its equivalent for women married to citizens, the *stola* – was worn on appropriate public occasions.

Whenever citizens entered the forum in Rome – and in other cities across the empire – Augustus insisted they wear the toga; and also when visiting the theatre or attending religious festivals. Certainly at the big public games in the arena, citizens were expected to be properly dressed and sitting in their designated areas. Augustus himself always kept a toga handy in case he had sudden need of one for unexpected official business when he was otherwise relaxing.

The guests at the dinner Pliny writes about were all social equals – apart from the freedmen present – and yet the host made distinctions between them. So even within the strictly demarcated social rankings, there was often a pecking order.

Accidents of birth

It was common for slaves who gained their freedom to become Roman citizens. But they were barred from holding high office or joining the army. However, adoption by a member of the elite could pave the way for a freed slave to be elevated into the decurion or equestrian rank. It was even possible for descendants of such adopted freedmen to become senators.

Imperial slaves and freedmen, while lacking the titles and privileges of rank, often had access to the emperor and hence an influence beyond that enjoyed even by members of the senate. Pliny draws our attention to one such honoured freedman – and leaves us in no doubt about what he thought of such things:

You will think it a joke – or an outrage, but a joke after all – if you read this, which has to be seen to be believed. On the road to Tibur, less than a mile from Rome, as I noticed the other day, there is a monument to Pallas with the following inscription: "to him the senate decreed in return for his loyal services to his patrons, the insignia of a praetor, and the sum of fifteen million sesterces, but he thought fit to accept the distinction only".

Pallas was a freedman who had served as financial secretary to the emperor Claudius. Pliny describes him later in the letter as "dirt and filth", no doubt because of his servile birth, adding that it was better to laugh about these things "or such people will think they have really achieved something". In another letter, Pliny asserts that it was wholly dishonourable of Pallas to refuse the money. Truly, honour is in the eye of the beholder.

Under marching orders

The Roman empire was at its heart a military dictatorship. It was born of victory in the civil war that erupted when Julius Caesar was assassinated. The eventual victor, who had started as Julius's adopted son, Octavian, and emerged as the all-powerful Augustus, owed his victory to the army.

And he paid his debt, because for the first time the world had a standing army at the behest of a powerful emperor. The army in the early empire numbered 250,000 men, two-thirds of whom were not needed to keep the peace on the borders or fight the wars of expansion in northern Europe.

So, the army was on hand to keep order. Its mere presence in the major cities of the empire ensured the run of the emperor's writ. For the first time regular soldiers, in the form of a 4,500-strong praetorian guard, were stationed in Rome. The guard became an elite force that was a centre of power in its own right through the first century, often influencing who occupied the highest office in the land, as when they compelled Claudius to become emperor following the removal of the increasingly mad Caligula.

In return, the legions were granted honours. They got special seating in the theatres and auditoria of the empire and upon retirement they were settled with land and honours in the various colonies that were established.

Soldiers served for twenty years – Augustus raising the length of service from sixteen years in AD 5. Because soldiers were not legally entitled to marry, the sons of the many unions that took place tended to join up, since as illegitimate children they had few prospects in civilian life. And so life in the legions became a sort of hereditary estate, with sons following fathers into uniform for many generations.

The standard pay of legionaries was 900 sesterces a year through most of the first century, with a 1,200 sesterces pay-off at the end of their service either in cash or in land. Veterans tended to migrate to places where former officers, members of the equestrian and decurion orders, might be able to offer them opportunities for preferment by serving as their clients.

See you at the club

There were associations of veterans that met to eat and reminisce. But you did not have to have served in the legion to join a club. As we saw earlier, voluntary associations of all kinds thrived in the early years of the empire, despite Augustus putting severe curbs on them. Such associations offered not only leisure activities but opportunities either to exercise patronage or to find a personal patron for a business venture or local advancement. They offered a way for ordinary people to feel that they were part of something, and thus that they were somebody.

Finding a place

People tend to think of the church as a religious organization. But it is not at all obvious that this is how the Romans would have seen the first Christians.

It is true that Pliny talks of the Christians "singing hymns to Christ as to a god" but the rest of his description of the Christian gathering in early second-century Pontus and Bithynia makes it sound more like a voluntary association than a cult.

And evidence from the New Testament suggests that the Romans saw the early church more as a political rather than religious club. The very name "Christian", which appears only three times in the New Testament, suggests this. What we have in Acts and 1 Peter is the Greek form of a Latin term created by adding the suffix –ianus to the name Christ. This was done for political groups, not religious ones.

It is clear from Acts 11:26 that the followers of Jesus did not hang the label "Christian" on themselves. It was given by their Roman neighbours. This is reinforced by the only other place that the word is used in Acts. In 26:28, when Paul is on trial before Festus and Agrippa, the representatives of imperial power in Judea, Agrippa declares in no uncertain terms that Paul will not persuade him to be a Christian. Although he later says to Festus that he does not think the movement is dangerous, joining it would not advance his career.

The only place in the New Testament where Christians adopt the term themselves is 1 Peter 4:16. Here Peter, writing in the mid-60s AD, a time of tension for the followers of Jesus, says to his hearers that, if they are accused of being a Christian, they should not be ashamed. In the context this can only really mean that although they have not chosen the label, it is not a bad one to have. He has already told them that their lives should be marked by good works that will silence the ignorant talk of foolish people (1 Peter 2:15).

The church seems to have functioned as a voluntary association, meeting to eat together and learn more about the movement's founder, Jesus. It is interesting that, when they were looking for a label to hang on their gatherings, they chose the Greek word *ekklesia*. It is the word from which we get our word "ecclesiastical" but in the first century it was not a religious term at all. It was a word used of assemblies of all kinds, but especially the citizen assemblies of Greek cities (see Acts 19:32–41), and also for gatherings of *collegia*.

What shall we call ourselves?

One of the most intriguing uses of the term in the New Testament is in Acts 19:39–41 where Luke tells us about a riot and a suggested lawful assembly. The word he uses for both is *ekklesia*. So, it seems that the early followers of Jesus chose a term that was familiar from ordinary life and sufficiently flexible for them to inject their own meaning into it.

In chapter 3 we saw how the group that met as church in Thessalonica could well have been a small gathering of similarly employed craft-workers. Indeed, the group might have looked to outsiders like a typical voluntary association of people from the same trade meeting in the name of a god (in their case Jesus) to eat together and offer mutual support.

When we add to this the fact that Paul did not want the believers in Corinth doing things that drew attention to themselves unhelpfully and suggested that the church was just another ecstatic eastern cult, a picture begins to emerge of the early church as looking like a voluntary association.

The words the early Christians chose to speak about their leaders also suggest that they saw themselves as a voluntary association as much as anything else. (It is an interesting question whether they were conscious of adopting any organizational model. They rather saw themselves as a family gathering in a home – see box "Greet the Family").

Despite being a Jewish movement, none of the language of synagogue leadership was used to talk about church leaders – with the exception of "elder", which we shall examine shortly – and this inspite of the fact that on at least one occasion a synagogue ruler was converted to the new faith (Acts 18:8). But when Crispus is mentioned in Paul's letters to the

Greet the Family

Reading Romans 16, it is apparent that Paul uses family language to describe fellow Christians who were not his relatives. He talks of loving various people, such as Ampliatus (16:8), and various individuals are his dear friends – Epenetus (16:5), Stachys (16:9), and Persis (16:12): the word he uses for each of these literally means "beloved" – and the mother of Rufus has also been a mother to Paul as well (16:13).

We see the language that was usually reserved for one's biological family being applied to the members of churches across the empire. These people, who had different backgrounds, came from various races, enjoyed varying levels of economic attainment, function as a family.

We see it even more clearly in 1 Corinthians 8 where Paul is talking about how members of the churches should treat each other. He is talking about the issue of meat bought in the market or eaten at a neighbour's house or in a temple at a voluntary association banquet. He is recognizing that different church members see this issue from different perspectives, almost certainly the result of occupying different levels of the prevailing social pecking order.

The way Paul makes his case is very simple. He reminds the Corinthians that they are a family. Four times in the concluding three verses of the chapter he talks about the person being offended as "a brother". And he does it where a simple pronoun would have sufficed because he wants to emphasize the close family link that is forged by common faith in Christ.

Indeed in his letters he uses the term "brother" 112 times. While it was not unknown for other Roman groups to use sibling language about one another, it is so frequent in Paul's case that it is clearly a key way that he understands the church.

And this matters because one's family was a key source and sustainer of one's social status. One's honour was acquired from one's family. Paul is saying that, regardless of their place on the social ladder, Christians get their status and honour from being part of the movement that is coalescing around Jesus, God's Son.

This idea is reinforced by Paul's use of adoption language in Romans. There he makes the startling claim that those who are led by the

Spirit of God are sons of God (Romans 8:14). When the first Roman believers heard this, they could well have been completely astonished.

There was a son of god in Rome already. He was Caesar. It was a title that Augustus had taken for himself early in his reign and it was handed on to each of his successors. And here was Paul saying that these ordinary people, these craft-workers, these social nobodies were sons of God because they had been chosen by the God and Father of their Lord Jesus Christ, who was *the* Son of God.

But more startling still is Paul's use of the language of adoption here. Each, bar one, of Augustus's first four successors, the Julio-Claudians, came to his exalted place as a result of being adopted by his predecessor, as Augustus had been adopted first by Julius Caesar. Here in these Roman tenements and workshops, in the back streets of the poorest quarters of the city, ordinary people were being adopted into a divine family, just as Caesar had been.

Here was a radical rewiring of notions of social status. Paul tells these ordinary working people that as followers of Jesus they are sons and daughters of a king, whatever their day job.

church, no reference is made to him retaining such a title in the church, though he does play a leadership role.

The three most common words for leaders in the churches of the New Testament were *diakonos* (servant, from which we get the word "deacon"), *presbuteros* (elder or old man), and *episkopos* (a term meaning overseer, from which we get our word "bishop"). The first and last of these were common terms for those with leading functions within voluntary associations. The middle term was used in the synagogues for those who led by virtue of their age and experience.

Paul's social status

As chapter 3 described, the wealthy elite looked down on those who worked with their hands. Indeed the author Plutarch says starkly: "while we delight in the work of craft-workers and artisans, we despise the worker . . . It does not necessarily follow that, if the work delights you with its graces, the one who wrought it is worthy of your esteem." And many philosophers boasted of knowing nothing of manual labour.

This makes Paul something of an enigma. Here is a literate, even literary, man, judging from the quality of his writing and thinking; a man familiar with and prone to quote poets and philosophers; a man who boasts the best education a Jewish father could buy his son; yet a man who works with his hands, a tent-maker. More than that, he urges his hearers to imitate his hard work.

What are we to make of him? In particular, where are we to locate him in the social pecking order described in this chapter?

It's the choices you make

Reading his letters to the churches at both Corinth and Thessalonica, it becomes clear that his manual work is not just a means of paying his way – though it is that – but a statement of intent about how the followers of Jesus should view the pecking order in the empire.

As a travelling teacher, Paul could have been supported by those he was teaching. He could either have charged for his lectures or received the patronage of a rich member of any congregation he was visiting. This appears to be what the churches in Corinth wanted. Those of means – a minority but still a significant and vociferous presence in the community – took umbrage that Paul not only declined their support but disgraced himself, and by implication them, by insisting on continuing at a trade.

In 1 Corinthians 9, Paul acknowledges this. He tells his Corinthian hearers that he could indeed have insisted that they support him but he has chosen not to because he wants the good news about Jesus to come free of charge to them, without strings attached – either by him or by the patrons who supported his visit.

He speaks to a group of people very concerned about their rights – their right to honour and status, in particular – and tells them that he is setting his rights to one side. Getting his due does not matter to him nearly as much as being able to pass on the gospel of Jesus.

Work is a good thing

Writing to the Thessalonian Christians, he makes much the same point, adding that his way of living is an example for them to follow.

We have already noted that this tiny church could well have still been meeting in the workshop in which it was born. It might have only consisted of a few craft-workers and maybe their families. When Paul had been with them, he had worked as they did. He had made tents, sold them, paid his way, and maybe paid the way of some who were not having as good a trading time as he was.

This is his theme in 1 Thessalonians 2:1–12. In 4:9–11, he applies his example to his hearers, urging them to work with their hands and be dependent on no one. It is possible that Paul has more in mind here than just encouraging his hearers to carry on working, as considered in the box overleaf ("Doing Good in the Community").

When he writes a second time to the church, however, he strongly reiterates the advice, saying that he did not eat anyone's food without paying for it (2 Thessalonians 3:8). This was simply because poor craft-workers could not afford to support idle wandering teachers. And so he encourages everyone in the church to do as he did, to work so they can eat and do good to others.

Again, Paul seems implicitly to be criticizing the culture that allows people to sponge off rich sponsors because they are adding to that patron's social standing. Paul will have none of this. As he said in 1 Thessalonians 4:11–12 we should be dependent on no one; part of our dignity comes from working with our hands, making something to sell so we can eat and can share what we have with those unable to work or down on their luck.

Doing Good in the Community

Because the early Christians were ordinary working people and there were not very many of them in each of the cities where the church was taking root, there was a temptation to opt for the quiet life and keep their heads down.

But the writers of the New Testament told them to do exactly the opposite. And intriguingly they were encouraged to use the very system the elite used to sustain their power to subvert the empire and make a world of difference for everybody in their neighbourhoods.

We see this very clearly in the letter Peter wrote to scattered communities in the towns and cities of what is modern-day Turkey. He knew they were facing pressure because he tells them not to be afraid if they are accused of being Christians.

But in 1 Peter 2:11–17, Peter says that, rather than keeping their heads down, the followers of Jesus should silence the foolish talk of their accusers by doing good works in their neighbourhoods. The language he uses in 2:14 is very similar to that which Paul uses in Romans 13:3–4. And the reason for this is very simple. This is the way people talked about benefactors in the community and especially the way such people °were noticed and honoured for the work they were doing.

So both Peter and Paul are arguing that, far from keeping a low profile, Christians should be doing things that get recognized by their neighbours as being worthy of commendation by the authorities.

As chapter 7 will note from a slightly different angle, this is what Paul is urging the Thessalonian believers to do. Some in that city are idle, says Paul: that is to say that these people were not working with their hands. Rather they were minding other people's business and depending on others for their daily needs (1 Thessalonians 4:11–12 and 2 Thessalonians 3:6–15).

What Paul is hinting at here is that these people were opting to be clients of patrons wealthier than they were who needed their support in the court and forum, needed them to run errands on their behalf and generally boost their honour by being seen supporting them.

Paul says this is no life for a Christian. Rather, he says, the followers of Jesus should be working with their hands so that they can be benefactors rather than clients – not people who act as patrons

➡️ because it brings them honour and prestige but people who do good in their communities because there is good that needs doing and doing it shows their neighbours something of the God they serve.

There is a very strong strand running through the New Testament that God's people should be doing good works. So in Galatians 6:10 Paul urges his hearers to do good to all, especially fellow believers, and in Titus 3:14, at the end of a letter that has had a considerable focus on the necessity of doing good works, the writer says, "Let people learn to do good works in order to meet urgent needs, so that they may not be unproductive." Clients of patrons are unproductive, but followers of Jesus who work with their hands and share what they have with those in need are anything but.

The New Testament writers argue that the Christian faith is a radical message: it can transform not only individual believers, but the world in which they live and work.

A key to success

This could be one of the key reasons why the Christian faith proved to be so attractive to the ordinary craft-workers who seem to have formed the core of the earliest churches we meet in the empire.

Here was a message about new life and hope being preached by a man who lived the same life that they did. Paul was not a rich, effete religious leader, offering advice on how to live the good life from the safety of a rich man's house. Rather he was a leather-worker, a tent-maker, who worked from sunrise to sunset with his hands to put bread on his table.

But more than that: this was the life he had chosen even though he had every right to earn his living by his preaching of the gospel (1 Corinthians 9:1–14). And this choice does two things simultaneously.

First, it elevates and gives enormous value to manual labour. If the bringer of a life-changing faith lives by manual work, it tells his hearers that this faith takes them and the lives they lead seriously.

And secondly, it calls into question the way society values people. Since it turns out that the founder of this faith was himself a carpenter for the majority of his life, then craft-workers across the empire suddenly find themselves at the same level as God incarnate. And the social pecking order, which kept them at the bottom of the heap lacking honour and status, is seen to be anything but the last word on the value of people in the eyes of God.

It was this upsetting of the social order that proved to be the enduring attraction of the Christian faith as it insinuated itself into the back streets of the empire.

CHAPTER 6

FAMILY LIFE

For most urban people, the family was the centre of their lives. The family home was where children began their education, where the elderly were cared for, and where (for most people) the work was done. The family home could well have been a crowded place. Uncles, aunts, and cousins rubbed shoulders through the day with slaves, freedmen, and clients. The crowded homes where the poor lived lacked any kind of privacy, while those of the wealthy were far more open to outsiders than homes in the western world today.

The church was born in such homes. And as people became followers of Jesus, so they had to think about the implications of their new faith for their family life in all its facets.

Laying the foundations

Cicero tells us how important the family was to the Romans:

Because the urge to reproduce is an instinct common to all animals, society originally consists of the pair, next of the pair with their children, then one house and all things in common. This is the beginning of the city and the seedbed of the state.

The proper functioning of the family was therefore essential to the happiness of individuals and the smooth running of society. For this reason, the Roman family was, in the eyes of the philosophers, a place of order and hierarchy. Legal opinion followed this view – though at a distance; and reality lagged a good way behind.

In theory and in law the father, the *pater familias*, was the head of the family, exercising the authority of an absolute monarch over everyone who lived under his roof – whether biologically related to him or not. This power was known as the *patria potestas*.

It meant that the Roman father was owner of all property in the household – even that of his adult children and anything a slave might earn doing business for him. Only he had the right to decide whom his children would marry. And he even had control over life and death: a baby born under his roof would not be received into the family until picked up and held aloft by the *pater familias*; on his say-so, it would be put outside to take its chance with nature and the kindness of strangers, the so-called exposure of infants.

The reality was that doting fathers were influenced by their children, and loving husbands were swayed by the opinion of their wives. Even more, the reality was that many *patres familias* died before being able to exercise much power, such was life expectancy in the empire (as we shall see).

Tying the knot

Marriage was the basis of family life in the empire. Roman marriage was created by the consent of a couple, a man and a woman. The state had no role in the creation of marriages – it did not even keep a register of them. And neither did religion play a significant role in weddings; although there were some religious rituals surrounding them, there was no religious service conducted by a priest of any kind.

The simplest way in which a marriage was created was by the couple living together for a year. At the end of this period everyone recognized that they were bound by marriage. In fact, what technically happened was that after twelve months the man assumed *manus* over the woman, as he would over any movable property that had been in his care for that period.

Manus means control, literally "hand". The *pater familias* exercised *manus* over all his property, including his children. He exercised this *manus* until his death, even over adult children, both boys and girls.

He could opt to release a child by an act of *emancipatio*, literally a sale to a third party, though it was usually marked by a ceremony rather than the handing over of money.

Manus over a daughter passed to her husband when she married. And the simplest way for this to happen was via a year's cohabitation. Normally, of course, the girl's family would have to consent, as would the girl herself. This way of marrying was more common among older women – late teenagers and those in their twenties.

The normal marriage age for girls was between twelve and sixteen. Weddings were arranged between families and involved negotiations over the bride's dowry and a ceremony involving both families. But even at this tender age, the bride and her groom – probably a good ten years older than she was – had to consent to the arrangement.

Naturally, this way of creating marriages applied to the elite and those in the cities who had a bit of income and aspired to be something in society. Often marriages were arranged to ensure that both families would benefit socially in the eyes of their neighbours.

The families of craft-workers and those scraping a living near the bottom of the social pecking order probably hoped their daughters would marry a skilled man. Maybe a daughter would be married off to an apprentice or the son of the family occupying the workshop next door. The truth is that scant records mean we know very little about marriage practice outside the elites.

Most marriages were marked by a ceremony and a party. Everyone likes a celebration, after all. And among the usual features of such ceremonies was the so-called "veiling of the bride". Often the veil in question was bright orange so no one present could miss the symbolism: from today this woman would be the wife of this man.

It was usual for married Roman women to wear the *stola*, a floor-length gown with sleeves or worn over a tunic – just as their husbands would wear the toga. These garments indicated their Roman citizenship and, for her, it showed the world she was married. Usually, when she went out, a married woman wore a *stola* and a *palla*, a shawl that she threw over one shoulder and drew up over the back of her head. This could well be significant when we read 1 Corinthians 11.

Drifting apart

Divorce was as straightforward as marriage in the early years of the empire. All that was needed was for the consent that cemented the marriage to break down. It was important for the families and friends of divorcing couples to be informed. Many divorces happened with good grace, perfectly amicably, with both parties walking away, free to form new liaisons.

Most separations were tricky, however, because of the children. Complications could also arise because of property, especially if the bride had brought a significant dowry into the marriage – her family would expect it, or the cash equivalent of it, back. This meant that, if they were still alive, the respective *patres familias* could get involved in the divorce, as they had been in the original wedding. It would be for them to agree the financial settlement, if any, as the couple parted.

Children of a failed marriage went to live with their father. He was their legal guardian and they were essential to ensure the continuation of his line. But mothers did not lose touch with their children. Both parties to the divorce might well get married again – the wife, almost certainly being younger than her husband, would definitely be expected to marry again and probably bear more children.

This meant that many Roman families were very complicated, with step-parents and step-siblings being extremely common. On top of that children might come into their mother or father's second marriage with a nurse or tutor in tow, who would join their counterparts in the new household.

Bundles of joy

Roman women had on average six or more children – they needed to because the mortality rate of infants under five was so high. Indeed each mother had to give birth to more than five children just to ensure the continuation of the husband's family line.

Romans seem to have loved their children, with both parents doting on them and both taking an interest in their development and education. We know this from the many tomb inscriptions that speak both lovingly and in detail of deceased children and infants.

That said, the richer the household, the more likely it was that the child would have been fed and looked after from the earliest days by a wet-nurse and would have had a tutor. Called a *paidogogus*, this slave was really more responsible for ensuring that the child (a boy, especially) did not get into trouble or go missing on forays outside the home than for organizing lessons.

Both the nurse and *paidogogus* very often would have spoken Greek to the child, again especially in the wealthier households. Greek was considered to be an essential component of a proper education and had been since the Roman world expanded to include the former empire of Alexander the Great.

Evidence of the high regard in which people held their families can be found in the works of philosophers and writers, and in the accounts of senate debates. In Tiberius's time, senators debated whether governors should take their families with them on overseas postings since these only usually lasted a year at a time.

No lesser man than Drusus, the emperor's grandson, extolled the virtues of taking the family along, arguing that husbands should not be forced to be separated from their wives and children, because of the pain it caused them. And his adopted brother Germanicus spoke of the deep pain of separation he had felt on being parted from his wife and children on a recent mission to Egypt.

Learn your lessons well

Education varied across the social classes. For the bulk of the population, it was pretty rudimentary. The children of craft-workers were probably helping out in their parents' workshops from an early age. If their father or mother could read – even to the extent of being able to decipher a bill of lading of some kind and maybe sign his or her name – then those skills would have been passed on. Otherwise, education would have consisted of learning the family business. Sometimes the eldest son of such families would be apprenticed to another craft-worker, or very occasionally to someone who would teach the child to write while he was trained to be a scribe or secretary.

There was no state education provided by the urban authorities, so elementary schools for seven- to eleven-year-olds tended to be run by literate men who were able to hire a shop or even mark out part of the forum and set up a classroom there. There was no furniture and no books. The teacher would sit on a large chair, with the children – often girls as well as boys – seated around him on the floor or benches. They would learn by rote, reciting back what the teacher said, writing it into wax boards using a metal stylus.

Many bright children of working people picked up a smattering of education – a bit of Greek, a facility with maths, the ability to frame a speech – from what they encountered in the city. They would hang about in the forum listening to the orators and the philosophers expound their latest theories. They might even eavesdrop on what was happening in the courts (since they too happened in the open air). They might catch a recital or drama on the steps of a temple during a festival and learn a few lines to entertain their parents after dinner.

For wealthier boys, elementary school led on to the secondary school. Every city had a few of these but many of the pupils at them would have been the sons of wealthy country people who were sent to lodge with relatives to further their education.

The teenage boys would learn philosophy, rhetoric, astronomy, geometry, and arithmetic, as well as music and the dramatic arts. It was book-based but, since there were very few books to go around, a passage would be read by the master and then explained. So that the pupils remembered, the texts would be repeated until memorized. Often they would have to write out extracts of texts on their boards and learn them that way.

Pliny

One of our major sources of information about how Romans saw the early Christians is Pliny the Younger. He was an equestrian who rose through the usual offices of state to become governor of the province of Pontus and Bithynia.

He was born in northern Italy in AD 62 to a relatively prosperous family but was adopted by his mother's brother, G. Plinius Secundus, a man we know as Pliny the Elder. This propelled the younger Pliny into the upper echelons of the Roman elite. When his uncle died in the eruption of Vesuvius that destroyed Pompeii in AD 79, Pliny inherited estates worth 400,000 sesterces a year.

Well educated, he joined the imperial service following a short stint in the army in Syria. Even while in uniform, he had found his niche – sorting out the finances of an auxiliary unit. Everywhere Pliny went he brought a keen accountant's eye and occupied many of the offices of Roman government that oversaw municipal and imperial finances.

He made his way through the *cursus honorum* fairly quickly, holding the high office of consul before his fortieth birthday. One of his proudest moments was when in AD 103 he was appointed to the office of augur. He wrote to a friend: "I have reached the same priesthood and consulship at a much earlier age than Cicero did. I hope I may attain something of his genius, at least in later life."

But he was still ambitious. He wanted to be provincial governor, pretty much the highest office someone in his position could attain. And he was not disappointed. In 109 Trajan appointed him as his personal legate to Pontus and Bithynia.

Pliny was a prolific letter-writer. Over 350 of his letters, 121 of them to his imperial employer, survive. And their survival was not an accident. He bundled them up into collections for posterity. And they provide us with a glorious and detailed portrait of a Roman gentleman at work and leisure, and a governor fulfilling his office with care and diligence.

Having been sent as Trajan's right-hand man to the far corner of the empire, one of his primary tasks was to sort out municipal finances. His letters, written as he travelled through his domain, inform us of how he set about this task in the cities of Prusa and Nicomedia, Sinope and Amisus.

➡️ Administration in this part of the empire did need some sorting out. There had been unrest and 0mismanagement. In particular, there was nervousness about the activities of local associations, *hetairiai*. Pliny wound up a few and, on the advice of Trajan, did not allow any new ones to be established.

And it is in the context of such associations that Pliny writes to Trajan about the activities of the Christians, a group he refers to as a *hetairia*. We learn from Pliny that the followers of Jesus were not that popular in the cities under his watchful eye. Their neighbours viewed them with suspicion, probably because they kept themselves to themselves and did not join in the local religious festivals. On top of that, most Christians seemed to come from the ignorant lower orders.

The people of the region were sufficiently concerned by their presence to have produced a pamphlet naming supposed followers of Jesus. Pliny viewed this new movement as most of his peers did, as a superstition and a foreign cult, and was in no doubt that the followers of it ought to be executed.

His letters give us invaluable insight into all this and constitute a unique window into the world of the early church.

Trained for imperial service

The sons of the elite – and a very few rich non-elite boys – went on from secondary school to learn rhetoric at a *schola* or lecture hall. The key lessons here were about the art of making speeches. After all, many of them would be making speeches for a living, either in courts of law or the various senates across the empire. But in the course of learning how to put fine oratory together, they would also learn the dominant philosophical traditions of the day. Some would learn other specialist skills such as architecture and engineering or shorthand and law. Some trained to be doctors, though medicine was not an elite profession. However, opportunities to undertake such training were scarce and often would-be doctors would have to travel to find a teacher who would take them on.

But most young people in the empire would never be involved in imperial service. Most would be ruled by the sons of the elite and live their lives on their wits and the few skills they had acquired from their parents or relatives.

It raises the question of how many people across the empire could read in the first century. The answer is that probably a lot could read a few letters. A character in a story by Petronius boasted that he had never learned geometry and literature and all the rest of that nonsense but he could read the letters on an inscription, knew his weights and measures, and could add up any sum. These were the skills a trader or craft-worker needed. They were sufficient to make a living in the empire's markets and workshops.

Most were not literate enough to read a book or a letter. So when the early Christians communicated with each other, they relied on the fact that in each gathering there would be someone with sufficient reading ability to read aloud the letter that had arrived from Paul or Peter. For most people, faith came by hearing, as Paul says in Romans 10. But that was good enough. In an oral culture, people did not need to hear things very often to remember them.

Live long and prosper?

Life in the cities of the Roman empire was hard and often very short. Average life expectancy at birth across the empire as a whole was around twenty-five; in the cities it was probably nearer twenty. But this did not mean that most people actually died in their twenties. Half of all babies died before their fifth birthday, but of those who reached the age of ten, half lived to fifty and a third made it to sixty. This means that less than a sixth of the population made it to sixty years of age.

Half of all children lost a parent or a nurse – an adult almost as significant to them as a parent – by the time of their tenth birthday. And a third of Roman children lost their father before they reached puberty. By that time nearly every child had witnessed the death of two or three brothers and sisters.

Roman homes were full of people. But the likelihood was that if three generations lived in the same home, the surviving grandparent would have been the grandmother. This is because women married on average ten years younger than men and had children almost immediately.

Since women were married in their mid-teens, it is likely that if one had given birth to healthy sons and daughters, and a daughter had married and taken her into her home or brought her new husband to the family home, then she would have been a grandmother in her mid- to late thirties.

By that time, her husband would have been in his mid- to late forties or older. The chances are that he might not have lived that long.

What a mixture

But there were other reasons why a child might grow up in a home without a grandfather. Divorce meant that families tended to fragment. It resulted in the Roman *familia* being a rich mixture of generations and relationships.

If the father and mother had divorced while the children were young, they would normally have stayed with the father. If he had remarried, his children would have gained a stepmother. She could well have come into the family home with some children of her own and possibly her mother. It is equally possible that the man's mother would have moved in when the divorce happened in order to help with child care.

When children were born to the second wife, those of the first marriage would often have taken a role in the care of their step-siblings. But they would also still have contact with their own mother and wet-nurse.

Roman families were complex and fragile.

Life under one roof

Roman homes were not only crowded, they were not very private places either. As described in chapter 3, most people worked at home. This meant that wherever they lived – whether it was a well-appointed *domus* or a couple of rooms behind a workshop or an apartment in an *insula* – people were coming and going all the time.

Customers, colleagues, clients, curious neighbours, government weights and measures men and other officials, not to mention various hangers-on, would drift in and out of the home through the day. On top of that, work was going on – even in the atria of well-appointed homes, spinning and weaving, sometimes on a commercial scale, was happening through the day.

The domestic realm was not really private. There were parts of the home that visitors did not go to – such as the bedrooms and slaves' quarters in the wealthier houses – but most of life was lived under the gaze of strangers and with the constant comings and goings of people from very early in the morning until late into the night. And this has to be borne in mind when thinking about what it was like for the churches gathering in such homes.

Homes – even pretty low down the social scale – were decorated to impress visitors. There were paintings on the walls of dining-rooms and in the *tablinum*, where the master of the house would receive clients and conduct business. There were mosaic floors in all but the most private of rooms. Curtains and statues, pots and plates were on show everywhere you looked.

And even those with little money tried to ape the style of the rich in what they had in their homes. In particular, the kind of art that rich people commissioned was copied by those lower down the social scale. Houses that have been excavated in Pompeii and Ostia, Ephesus and Pergamum indicate that, at all levels, what your home looked like mattered to most people.

The home was the centre of most people's lives in the Roman empire. And it is clear that families wanted to show them off. They wanted their homes to be full of people – relatives and visitors, customers and clients – because they wanted neighbours from near and far to think well of them.

Housefuls of the holy

The home was also the centre of the religious life of the family. As will be explained in chapter 8, every household had gods (*lares*) sited in a *lararium* (a shelf or open cupboard containing one or more statuettes) within the family home. The *pater familias* would normally have led the family each morning in a simple act of devotion, seeking the protection of the *lares* for his family through the day. The act would have been accompanied by offerings of incense or food.

Everyone in the home would have worshipped the same god as the master. It was rare to find members of the same family following different household gods, although outside the home, independently chosen membership of a cult was possible for any family members.

So the home was a place of work and worship, fun and feasting. It was the centre of life, where most members of the household spent most of their time. It was the key venue where everyone learned the values by which they would live in the world outside the home. It was the source and centre of their identity. It was the most important place in the empire.

Clustering around the table

So it seems entirely appropriate that it was in the homes of the early followers of Jesus that the movement took shape. Paul writes to a group of Christians in Corinth whose regular habit was to gather in various homes across the city – the homes of Chloe (1 Corinthians 1:11), Stephanas (1 Corinthians 16:15–17), and Gaius (Romans 16:23), and almost certainly others.

Historians are divided on what kinds of homes these groups met in. Some argue that they must have been the homes of well-to-do Corinthians, since Paul talks about social divisions within the church and mentions believers who were able to make use of the courts to settle disputes (access to the courts was restricted to those with money). So they envisage these small churches gathering around the dining-table in the triclinium of a well-appointed *domus*.

Others argue that since the Corinthian believers we know about were craft-workers – people such as the tent-makers Aquila and Priscilla – they would have lived in rooms at the back of their workshops or at best in apartments in *insulae*. The meals they shared would not have been served in dining-rooms by household slaves but eaten in the one room that the host family occupied, with everyone sitting on the floor or on the bales of cotton and leather awaiting manufacture into a tent or awning.

Eating and learning

It is most likely that a majority of the Corinthian believers were not well off and they lived in *insulae* or workshops, but a small minority of the church does seem to have consisted of people of means, who might well have hosted the gatherings of believers. We have to imagine Paul's words being heard by groups in both kinds of venue – some reclining in a dining-room, possibly with an overspill in the atrium, and others squeezed into workshop or apartment.

But his words were being heard in places that were busy and brimming with people, some of whom were not followers of Jesus, not there for the gathering of the church at all. Rather they had dropped by to place or collect an order, to pay their respects to a patron, to deliver raw materials for tomorrow's work. Some might have been visiting the home of relatives because they had come to the city on business. Some might be the guests of the host, who had invited them along to find out what the Christian faith was all about because they had already talked about it on another occasion.

What we know for sure is that food was involved in the gathering. If it happened in the workshop, then the scene Paul talks about in 1 Corinthians 11:17–34 happened at the end of the working day, with everyone bringing something to share. It is possible that the home owner has gone out and got wine and vegetable stew from the local *popina*, while someone else has been sent to buy bread, which at the end of the day might be cheaper than first thing as it is going stale. Maybe everyone, except the very poorest among them, has brought something.

If the scene is a *domus*, then we can picture the host providing the basics of a meal – especially wine for the symposium – with some others bringing dishes to share. An evening meal in a *domus* would have started quite a bit earlier than the end of the working day. The wealthy tended to begin a leisurely meal in the late afternoon. Any working people in their group would have arrived late when the meal was already in full swing.

This could be why Paul says that some of the diners are arriving when there is no food left, while others who have been there a while have already eaten and drunk too much.

Is there a dress code?

Because churches met in homes and gathered people from different social levels as well as different families, did it matter how people dressed? The previous chapter mentioned how only certain people were able to wear purple on their clothes. And we saw earlier in this chapter that Roman citizens wore the toga and *stola* when out in public to show their status and place in society.

So did the rules about how married women dressed when they were in public apply to a gathering in someone's home? Paul thought they did and in a somewhat difficult passage he seems to be suggesting that dress and behaviour in church are closely linked and that everyone attending ought to be careful about the signals they are sending out by how they dress.

He draws attention to two things in particular. First, he says that men should not cover their heads when praying. The practice he seems to be referring to here is that of elite men drawing their togas up over their heads when they were leading public prayers or offering sacrifices (see chapter 8 for details).

It appears that some men in the Corinthian churches were doing that when they prayed in church, thus showing that they had pretensions to high social status. In effect, they were saying to the rest of the congregation, "I am better than you." This, says Paul, is hardly appropriate behaviour when praying in church, where everyone is equal before God.

Secondly, he says that married women, when they are praying or bringing a word of prophecy, should signal their marital status by wearing their *palla* or shawl drawn up on the back of their heads.

Does my head look big in this?

He probably does this for two reasons. The first is that he does not want other male worshippers to get the wrong idea about the women taking part in the service. In Roman religion, female priests and prophets were powerful figures. And power and sexual allure are close cousins.

Later in this section, he says that it is not good if the church's worship gives the impression of everyone being wild and ecstatic (1 Corinthians 14:23). He is not saying that anyone happening to come into the room at that moment would think they were all mad. Rather, they would think that their faith was just like that of the various mystery cults, such as those of Isis and Dionysus, which were particularly attractive to women and were marked by frenzied styles of worship (see chapter 8 for more details). Unveiled married women might give that impression and lead visitors to think that Christianity is just another mystery cult.

The second reason he gives concerns "the angels" (1 Corinthians 11:10). This Greek word means ordinary human messenger as well as heavenly being and Paul could well have in mind the people coming and going from the meeting who might carry a message about the conduct of the service to neighbours or people in authority.

Magistrates were charged with responsibility to ensure that the social dress code was observed. They could stop men who were not citizens from wearing the toga. And they would take a dim view of married women being improperly dressed while they took part in a public assembly. They would already have had their doubts about the Christian meetings as it was. Paul is keen that the church does nothing unnecessary to add to their fears.

Do I know you?

Paul is very aware that not everyone at the Christian symposium would be a follower of Jesus. It is not only the reference to messengers in 1 Corinthians 11:10, but also the one to those who just happen by in 14:24.

He is probably referring to any number of people who could be at the meeting. They might be household servants or slaves of the host and hostess who are not Christians but who are serving the meal. They could be clients of the householder who have come to pay their respects to their patron.

They could be neighbours or business contacts of the householder who have been invited to share the meal and conversation of the symposium with a view to telling them something about the new teaching they are following. They could be the spouses of worshippers who are not yet believers (Paul mentions them in 7:12–16).

Paul is aware that all kinds of people could drift in and out of the gathering and he wants nothing that happens there to cause a scandal or prevent them seeing and hearing something of the Christian message in a way that makes them wonder whether it might be for them.

Cut the noise at the back!

And it could be for this reason that Paul ends the section where he began it – with the wives of those attending. In 1 Corinthians 14:34–35 he suggests that women – he probably has wives of men who are also present in mind – should not talk in the gathering. But since he has said in 11:2–16 that they can pray and prophesy, providing, if they are

What's in a Name?

Roman families were desperately keen to see their name descend down the generations. So Romans had at least three names – the *tria nomina* – though many added more to take account of the mother's family and the names of great houses to which they were attached through patronage.

The *praenomen*, usually written as just a capital letter, was one of seventeen or so names used by 99 per cent of Roman males. So, T. is for Titus and L. for Lucius. It was the name that parents and friends would use to address the person.

The *nomen* was the family or clan name. This was the most important part of your name because it told people who your ancestors were and indicated whether your origins and current status were patrician or plebeian. So names such as Julius, Claudius, etc., were carried by all male members of the family whatever their *praenomen*. There were female equivalents of these names given to daughters: Claudia for the daughter of a Claudius, Julia for Julius's.

And the *cognomen* distinguished various branches of a family or clan as the number of descendants from a single original family multiplied. These were names such as Paullus, Gracchus, and Maximus. Many of these names seem to have been derived from nicknames. So Pulcher means "handsome" and Verrucosus means "warty".

How do you tell them apart?

So there are, for example, many generations of M. Claudius Marcellus (the M. standing for Marcus), descendants of a man, the first known holder of the name, who was one of Rome's two consuls in 183 BC. Each of these bearers of the same name held high office in the city through to and beyond the first century AD.

One assumes their mothers and grandmothers could tell them apart, and more importantly, they knew who was meant when one of them called "Marcus"!

Second sons were given a different *praenomen*. So M. Claudius Marcellus's younger brother was G. (for Gaius) Claudius Marcellus.

Slaves had a single name followed by the name of their owner. But when a slave gained his freedom, he took on the name of the family that had once owned him. So an inscription in Rome tells us about married, they are properly dressed, this cannot be a prohibition on their taking part in the meeting.

It is likely that what he has in mind is wives asking their husbands questions, possibly about what is going on in the gathering but possibly about other matters that have nothing to do with the symposium. Paul suggests that they wait until they get home, when they will have their husbands all to themselves.

Paul was not unique in issuing such advice. Many of the inscriptions that contain the rules governing the operation of voluntary associations take a dim view of guests who talk while they are supposed to be listening. And some of the Roman moralists took exception to the wives of guests talking to them about family business rather than paying attention to the topic of the symposium. Plutarch, speaking generally about conduct at such gatherings, speaks of how ill-mannered it is when people talk out of turn or ask questions that clearly indicate that they have not understood what the speaker has been saying.

Paul's desire was that the Christian symposium should be a place where people of both sexes could freely express themselves in an atmosphere of mutual respect. It seems that something of the competitive spirit for which Corinth was infamous had crept into the church and that was taking attention away from the subject under discussion.

It is interesting that Paul opens and closes this section on the conduct of the symposium with reference to the behaviour of women. There was clearly an issue about this at Corinth and while he was keen for both sexes to participate on an equal footing – after all, some of his best leaders and teachers were women – he was equally keen that nothing happen in the gathering that would discredit the Christian movement in the eyes of the wider world.

Following Jesus at home

People who had become Christians had all kinds of questions about how this new faith affected the way they lived at home with their families. We know this because many New Testament passages touch on it.

In 1 Corinthians 7 we read all about sexual ethics and whether or not it was a good idea to get married in the light of the difficult economic circumstances in the mid-50s AD. Ephesians 5 and Colossians 3 offer advice on household relationships to those who lived in such households – obviously not everyone was covered by the relationships treated in these passages.

Augustus's reforms favoured the elite over everyone else. But not everyone was thrilled to see them enacted. Many young elite men resented being told to get married because it cramped their lifestyle, forcing them to settle down before they were ready to do so.

But for ordinary people the concerns of family life were much more basic: will we be able to afford to get married? Is having another child sensible when that means another mouth to feed when money is already tight?

These sorts of questions lie behind Paul's wide-ranging treatment of the topic of marriage in 1 Corinthians 7. It was sparked by a question the church had asked of him that had something to do with the idea that it was good for the married to abstain from sex and for those looking forward to tying the knot to put their plans on hold.

Paul agreed that there was a current crisis (7:26), probably food shortages that blighted the city through the 50s. But even so, marriage was important. So he says two key things in a section that ranges across a number of topics in this area.

Give yourselves to each other

The first thing he says is that marriage is for having sex and that couples should not deny each another. His teaching is fairly radical in that he

Augustus, Paul, and Sex

When he had consolidated his grip on power, Augustus was concerned to address the lax morals of Roman citizens. He passed a number of laws regulating sexual behaviour, with the intention of boosting the birth rate and bolstering Roman marriage.

For example, the sex lives of Romans were regulated for the first time with prohibitions on sex outside marriage between elite people; senators and their descendants were not allowed to marry prostitutes, stage performers, or freedwomen, and women could be tried for adultery (though not men).

Incentives to have children were introduced. It was expected that men would be married by the time they were twenty-five, preferably earlier, so that they could sire children. An elite man was allowed to subtract one year from the minimum age at which he could become an office-holder for each child born to his wife.

Freeborn women with three children, and freedwomen (that is, those who had started out in life as slaves but had gained their freedom) with four children, were freed from guardianship. This meant that they could hold property in their own right and it did lead to a number of instances where women were able to become successful in business and earn a good living.

treats men and women equally. Now Roman law would argue that the wife belongs to the husband but Paul adds that the husband equally belongs to the wife (1 Corinthians 7:2–4).

In this he seems to go even further than the idealistic Rome-based stoic philosopher Musonius Rufus, who said:

The husband and wife . . . should come together for the purpose of making a life in common and of procreating children, and furthermore of regarding all things in common between them, and nothing peculiar or private to one or the other, not even their own bodies.

The second thing Paul says is that, even though it is sensible to put off enterprises that might stretch already scarce resources to breaking-point, that should not be made to apply to marriage where both parties are keen to go ahead (7:36–40 – though it should be noted that there are a number of issues with the language Paul uses here that make translation difficult).

Use power with grace

Elsewhere in his letters Paul is keen to ensure that those with power in the household use it in a way that reflects the character of Christ. In the so-called household codes of Ephesians 5 and Colossians 3, Paul addresses the three key household relationships – husband and wife, father and children, master and slave. We need to note two things here.

The first is that the first person in each pair is the same person, the *pater familias* of the house, who had absolute rights of control over all other members of the household. What is noteworthy is that Paul does not address the man first. Rather he addresses the wife, the children, and the slave first, thus indicating that he treats them as equals with the *pater familias*.

The second thing to note is that he expects far more of the husband/father/master than he does of the others in the relationships. After all, law and custom dictate that wives, children, and slaves must obey their *pater familias*.

So Paul is more concerned to ensure that the husband loves and treats his wife with equality and respect, that the father gives the most supportive upbringing to his children that he can, and the master treats slaves with dignity. Indeed with regard to the latter relationship, some have suggested that the letter to Philemon argues that Christian masters should give their slaves their freedom.

CHAPTER 7

MAKING ENDS MEET

The economic circumstances of most people in Roman cities were balanced on a knife-edge. In good times, most people made enough each day to get by – namely, to eat and pay their rent. In bad times hunger and homelessness were very real dangers for thousands of citizens.

The landowning elite, however, lived comfortably, even lavishly. They had country estates, farmed by thousands of slaves and managed by trusted freedmen, and well-appointed city villas, run by a coterie of slaves and household retainers.

But beyond that, how the economy of the early Roman empire actually worked is a matter of some debate among historians. And that debate is important for the study of the Christian communities in the cities of the first century, because having a clear picture of the economy helps us place these first followers of Jesus in their proper social context.

In particular, the debate centres on whether there were people in the empire's cities who lived between the two extremes outlined above, who made enough money to eat well, live in a home with some decoration and durables, educate their children, and have a surplus that would have enabled them to get through a lean time.

An empire of farmers

One view of the Roman empire holds that virtually all the wealth was in the hands of a tiny minority of the population and it was tied up in land. The rich were not interested in increasing their net worth through investing in manufacturing, mining, or trade because their farms and lands generated all the wealth they needed – a wealth that was growing very nicely through the first century. As for the rest of the population, they lived at or around subsistence, living hand-to-mouth lives that were a constant struggle for food and warmth.

This view suggests that the economy was solidly agrarian. Food production rose to meet demand, especially for grain, olives, and grapes for wine. But large-scale manufacturing and trade in goods across long distances was not attractive to those with money; they had no interest in investing in making or moving things and so a brake was put on economic innovation.

The simple reason for this was that ownership of land was the basis of elite power. There was, therefore, no incentive for those with money to risk it in a speculative venture in manufacturing or trade. For example, putting money into the ships that brought grain to the major cities of the empire, especially Rome, was very uncertain because of the number of shipwrecks and lack of insurance on cargoes lost at sea. So why risk it when the same amount invested in more land would offer a guaranteed return? Indeed, most of the historians who hold this view of the Roman economy argue that such trade was an imperial monopoly, run by state officials, with no place for any kind of private enterprise.

Land is power

Landowners had political power for the simple reason that the people who paid them rent or worked their land – the vast majority of the population – gave them that power by supporting their claims to public office. Every time the landowning elite bought another 100 acres, they acquired all the tenants who farmed that land and added them to their coterie of supporters and clients.

And because landowners dominated the political landscape, those few urban people making money through manufacturing or trade ploughed their profits into buying land in the hope that their families would eventually be elevated into the ruling elite. For this reason, there was little incentive to invest in manufacturing or trade, so there was very little innovation in new, more efficient and large-scale ways of making and shipping goods throughout the whole period of the Roman empire (over 400 years).

Cities, according to this argument, were places of consumption rather than power-houses of wealth creation. They were where the wealthy elites consumed what was produced elsewhere – namely in the countryside. So there is evidence, for example, that the cities of Sepphoris and Tiberias in Galilee did not manufacture any of their own pottery. Rather they bought it in from small-scale producers in the villages of rural Galilee along with agricultural produce that came into the cities' markets.

This view is reinforced by the rather dismissive attitude of most Roman writers, seeing trade and making things as very low-status activities, and certainly not something with which the rich, elite readers of their works should be sullying their hands (see box, p. 147).

A vibrant market economy

But there is another view of the Roman economy that argues that cities of the size that many had reached in the first century could not have been sustained without a lively market in all kinds of goods and services, offering abundant opportunity for enterprising non-elite people – especially the recently freed skilled slaves of the ruling orders – to make a good living and accrue tidy sums of money.

Indeed, there is a lot of evidence that the elite supported traders and manufacturers by their patronage – putting money into workshops, investing in shipping companies, buying the products produced by their former slaves. In return for this, these rising urban folk gave their support to the political aspirations of their patrons.

This meant that the power-base of the elite was bolstered by urban occupations as well as by land ownership. So, for example, Plutarch tells us that the senator Cato the Elder took a one-fiftieth share in a trading company that was hiring ships to bring grain to Rome. We do not know for sure whether this was just for a single voyage, after which the company was split up and the profits divided among the "shareholders", or a permanent association that continually hired ships to bring goods to the capital from all over the empire.

And he was not alone in seeing that there was good money to be made from investing in trade. Of course, the elite would not actually run such businesses. Rather they would use a slave or a freedman who was still a client to front the business on their behalf – and, having put up the capital to finance the business, they would take the lion's share of the profits.

Simply feeding the cities, so this argument goes, would have created opportunities for people to make money through shipping and other transport services, warehousing grain and other foodstuffs, splitting bulk consignments into quantities that householders would have wanted to buy at the market. And, because the government was not large enough to do the job, such trade could not have been an exclusive imperial monopoly. So government officials might have overseen it and ensured that the merchants brought enough food into the cities – especially Rome – but much of the day-to-day trade would have been in the hands of private businessmen.

On top of this, there needed to be a ready supply of cash to invest ahead of the time when the boats arrived, the goods were sold, and the profits made. In other words there needed to be a rudimentary banking system. And evidence from Pompeii and elsewhere suggests that there were people who made a good living by lending money at interest to people involved in overseas trade and other business activities.

A perplexing blend

In all likelihood the Roman economy was a mixture of the two views outlined above. Yes, the elite did maintain their power by investing mainly in land and this did put a brake on innovation in trade and manufacturing. Yes, a large proportion of the rural workforce were slaves, which did depress rural wages. At the same time, however, the needs of those same elite people – for homes that displayed their high status, clothes that made them look the part, and food to ensure they could entertain well – meant that there was opportunity for all kinds of small-scale craft-workers, manufacturers, and traders to make a living supplying their needs.

And though the economy depended on slavery – especially in the rural areas – the evidence is that during the first century wage rates were not depressed by the numbers of slaves, suggesting that there were not enough enslaved people to do all the work that needed doing.

The evidence is certainly overwhelming that the cities of the empire were places bustling with gainful activity. Inscriptions tell us that market-days were regular – weekly in small cities, almost daily in most large ones – suggesting a constant supply of agricultural produce for sale. Comparison of the inscriptions from cities close to each other, in Greece for instance, indicates that different cities held markets on different days, allowing the same suppliers and growers to bring their goods to more than one place.

Such markets, though mainly concerned with foodstuffs, would also have sold pots for daily and decorative use, and items made of wood and metal for use around the home that were manufactured in the same places that the food was being grown.

Most peasants, who did not live in cities, lived within walking distance of one. It is estimated, for instance, that most rural Italians were between eleven and thirteen kilometres from their nearest city or market-town. This enabled them to visit urban areas perhaps a couple of times a week when they had produce to sell. Markets in cities commanded higher prices than those achieved selling the same produce at the farm gate, giving smallholders the incentive to get their goods to market. Often they would form associations to acquire a cart and pack animal for the purpose.

Middling sort of people

So the question is, was anyone making any money from all this activity, other than the tiny number of elite people who ruled the empire?

Some answer with a very firm "no", saying that the empire consisted of two groups separated by a vast gulf, a so-called "hour-glass-shaped" economy. One was the tiny minority of wealthy people – perhaps between 1 and 3 per cent of the entire population of the empire – who controlled the vast majority of wealth. The other was the rest, who lived at or around subsistence level, earning just enough to get by if they were lucky, going without food or shelter in the hard times.

And it was slavery that kept the non-elite free people in poverty. Without the presence of so many slaves in the economy, wage rates would have been higher and there would have been more jobs for free people to do in agriculture and domestic service, for instance.

But the evidence suggests that this is too simplistic a view of life in Rome's cities. So an increasing number of historians are working to identify the kinds and numbers of people who might be said to have occupied the middle ground.

And this matters for a proper understanding of the early church because the New Testament seems to suggest that it was precisely from such a middling group that the core members – and especially the leaders – of the first Christian communities came.

Those historians who provide evidence for a vibrant economy in the first century argue that it was craft-workers and small traders who made it so. For instance, thousands of examples of household goods bearing images of the imperial family have been unearthed across the empire. In countless homes, oil lamps, bowls, roof tiles, signet rings, even the Roman equivalent of piggy banks, have been found bearing the symbols of the divine Caesars. These finds presuppose workshops turning out such manufactured goods and, in the absence of large-scale manufacturing, such workshops would have been small and very local.

In Pompeii historians have identified more than fifty ways of making a living, from weaver to gem-cutter, potter to metalworker, architect to pastry-cook, barber to public pig-keeper. They have even found graffiti referring to a woman called Faustillia, who operated as a pawnbroker, lending money on goods at a rate of 3 per cent per month.

Many of these people would have been earning sufficient each week to pay for their food and housing, buy some goods to adorn their homes – maybe some sticks of furniture, a few pots, a wall-hanging to brighten their main room – and have a bit of a cushion against a week or two of bad trading conditions. And these people, in turn, were spending a little of their surplus on modestly priced manufactured goods made locally or shipped in from further afield which were made by other small-scale craft-workers like themselves.

In short, there was a modest market for what we might call consumer goods, as well as a larger market for the essentials of life – especially food and clothes. In Rome there was even a shopping precinct where such goods would have been sold. Rome had always had various markets selling all kinds of goods. But in the reign of the emperor Trajan (AD 98–117), a 170-room six-level structure was built against the slope of the Quirinal hill to house a multi-storey market. Trajan built it to clear the traders from the site of his new forum (the central town square, which was the political, religious, and social hub of the city). Given the rents that would have been charged for retail space in such a prime location, there was clearly money to be made selling goods to people of all kinds in the city.

Occupying the middle ground

But how many people were there in this group that was neither part of the elite nor struggling to make ends meet at the bottom of the pile? It is impossible to be sure, but the best guess is that maybe a third of the urban population occupied this middle ground.

This was a mixed group of people, to be sure. Some lived just above subsistence but were secure in terms of food and shelter. Others were better off, being able to own or rent a comfortable place to live, to have food enough to entertain and a regular small surplus enabling them to buy goods to decorate their homes.

Two groups in particular have been identified who might occupy this middle ground alongside the craft-workers who were able to turn their skills into a good living. The first are known as the *apparitores*.

This was a substantial group of literate men, whose name literally means "servants", appointed to work for civic magistrates in all branches of local government, as scribes, heralds, and messengers. They often gained their positions through patronage – perhaps they were the freedmen of an office-holder – but they retained them through skill and experience.

These were upwardly mobile, educated people, able to use their skills to serve the various members of the ruling elite who held the multiple administrative offices in cities across the empire. Their position in society was entirely dependent on the service they rendered, but through it many were able to accrue significant material rewards. They were not rich and would never be part of the elite but they were comfortably off.

The second were the *Augustales,* a group of mainly freedmen who enjoyed the patronage of elite families and were engaged in a variety of civic activities, some of which could have involved running business organizations – such as shipping and manufacturing operations – which were owned by those elite families. *Augustales* got their name by being part of a *collegium* of trusted former slaves who had a role in the imperial cult, organizing sacrifices on the appropriate days through the year, and games, often in honour of Caesar's birthday. Such a role would probably have lasted a year – as did most public offices – and would have been directed by the members of the local elite who served as priests in the cult (see chapter 8 for more details).

Their wealth would have come from the businesses they ran on behalf of their elite patrons. It fitted them to be part of the decurion class from which local magistrates were drawn, but the *Augustales* could not serve in such a capacity because of their servile past. However, their spending could rival that of their decurion neighbours.

Both *Augustales* and *apparitores* were men whose wealth exceeded their social status (see chapter 5) and so they found themselves in a slightly uncomfortable position in society. They had a considerable income, which separated them from the bulk of the urban poor, but they lacked the status that would have made them part of the elite. Thus both groups would have found the message of the Christian movement intriguing and attractive.

Paul's friends and associates

So, with this in mind, what do the accounts of the various people in Paul's circle tell us about their location in the economic pecking order? It is hard to be certain, but it is quite likely that the earliest Christian communities were unusual mixtures of the poor and of aspiring middle-order people who were making money in the relatively good economic circumstances of the early empire. There were probably very few who were completely destitute, and no members of the elite at this stage. But the Christian groups were unusual because most voluntary associations tended to consist of the same kinds of people. And because of their economic differences, they were each having to learn what being a follower of Jesus meant for their relationships with one another.

Having already met some of these people, it is now time to meet a whole group of them from one city – Rome – that we know about because of Paul's greetings to them at the end of his letter to the churches in that city.

Romans 16:1–16 is the longest and most detailed list of greetings in any of Paul's letters. In recent years it has been analysed closely for clues that will tell us about life in the Roman house churches and for any light it throws generally on Christian organizations themselves. Such analysis has yielded fascinating results.

It is possible that there are as many as seven house churches reflected in the list of names. Whether this is the total number of churches in the city, we have no way of knowing. These are only the ones known to Paul through his contacts – many of whom have worked with him in other places (Corinth and Ephesus, for example) and are now living in the capital.

So in 16:3–5 the house church of Aquila and Priscilla is identified, which probably also had Epenetus as a member. It is possible that they were the only couple in the city with a house (a *domus* or workshop with living accommodation attached). Others may have worshipped in churches based in *insulae*.

In 16:14 Paul greets five named individuals and the believers with them, suggesting a group that met regularly; and in 16:15, another five and the saints that met with them. It has been suggested that these two groups might have been people who met at work – in the workshop of one of them – or after work in a *popina* in one of the poorer areas of the city.

A real mixed bag

In 16:10b Paul greets those of the household of Aristobulus. Paul does not greet the householder, suggesting that he was not a Christian. Some in the household were, however – probably slaves or freedmen. It suggests a house of some wealth and tolerance – allowing members of the household freedom to belong to a cult to which the master did not belong.

It is possible that this Aristobulus was the grandson of Herod the Great and brother of the late Herod Agrippa. If so, he died in AD 44 and his household would have been united with the imperial household. So this church seems to have consisted of upwardly mobile administrators, *apparitores*, whose careers depended on loyalty to the emperor.

It is also possible that these Christian household slaves could have been one of the ways the Christian faith reached the capital sometime in the late 30s AD.

In 16:11 greetings are sent to some people in the household of Narcissus. The same applies here as above. Narcissus was not a Christian. He might have been Claudius's freedman, who died soon after his master: his household would have become part of Nero's household, as that of Aristobulus had done. Again this is a group of *apparitores* but, this time, a predominantly Gentile one.

In 16:6–9, twelve to fourteen other people are mentioned, many of them leading figures in the mission of the church. They do not seem to be attached to any of the churches so far mentioned. So do they constitute a sixth group or a sixth and seventh?

The mixture of groups identified above, all meeting in homes and workshops around the city, could well account for some of the problems

Junia and Andronicus

There are many names in the New Testament of people we apparently know nothing about. But a little judicious detective work can unearth a rich story behind a name or two.

For example, in the long list of greetings at the end of his letter to the churches in Rome, Paul mentions Junia and Andronicus, "my relatives, who were in prison with me; they are prominent among the apostles, and they were in Christ before I was" (Romans 16:7). These seem to be significant people and yet they are only mentioned here. Is it possible to put flesh on their bones after all this time?

The answer is probably "yes" for two reasons. The first is that Roman people generally had at least three names (see chapter 6) but New Testament writers only refer to one of them. And secondly, there is a well-attested tradition of people changing their names as they got involved with the Jesus movement. The most famous is Simon the fisherman, whom Jesus called Peter (which means "rock"); but there is also Joseph the Levite, whom the disciples renamed Barnabas, meaning "son of encouragement" (Acts 4:36), and Paul himself, who first enters Luke's story with the name Saul.

It was very common for Jewish people to have a Hebrew name by which they were known in their own community and another for the wider Roman world. This was probably the case with Saul/Paul. And it seems very likely to be the case with Andronicus and Junia.

And there was probably another reason why some in the early church operated with a number of names – safety. It was dangerous in some places and at some times to be a Christian. And some Christians, in particular those involved in taking messages between churches and those prominent in mission work, faced particular dangers.

Paul describes Junia and Andronicus as his relatives (by which he probably means fellow Jews rather than cousins or siblings) and people who have been Christians longer than he has. Since he had probably joined the movement within a year of the crucifixion and resurrection of Jesus, this couple must have been in the wider circle of Jesus' followers during his earthly ministry.

Now, Luke tells us about a significant group of women who travelled with Jesus and his disciples. Among them was one called Joanna, the wife of Chuza, Herod's steward (Luke 8:1–3). They followed Jesus from Galilee to Jerusalem and stayed with him even as he was dying on the cross (23:53). And they were the ones who brought spices to complete the burial rituals who were greeted by angels on the first Easter morning (24:1–12).

It is quite likely that Joanna and Chuza were socially prominent people for whom being Christians was something of a risk – especially given Herod's antipathy to Jesus. So as they got involved in the movement that arose in Jesus' name, they used different names: names that were more Latin-sounding. The change from Joanna to Junia is fairly obvious. Her husband, as a high-status Jewish man in the Romanized court of Herod Antipas, could well have had a Roman *trinomen* of which Andronicus was one part.

It is possible that this couple were part of the early community of believers in Jerusalem who were scattered when a wave of persecution swept over the church in the mid-30s AD following the stoning of Stephen. They could well have gone to Antioch and worked alongside Paul. It has been suggested that Andronicus was known as Manaen (which means "comforter" – named in Acts 13:1 as someone with close connections at Herod's court) while in Antioch, since using his real name in that volatile city could have made him a target.

They clearly travelled because they are in Rome when Paul writes to the churches there in the late 50s AD. Perhaps they travelled widely before reaching the capital. At some stage they shared a cell with Paul, and their work for the churches caused him to observe that they were "prominent among the apostles".

So, a story lurks behind every name.

---

that Paul has to address as he writes to the Roman Christians. It seems clear that there were ethnic differences among the Roman Christians – some were Jewish, others Gentile, most were migrants from other parts of the empire.

Money and manners

Some scholars have suggested that each of the congregations identified had a particular theological flavour.

So Priscilla and Aquila's church would have been solidly Pauline in theology – as the couple had worked for so long with Paul. It is likely, therefore, that it would have consisted of a racial mixture of Jew and Gentile, and women would have played a leading role.

The church in Aristobulus's household, because of its Herodian origins, would have been pro-Jewish and pro-Roman, nervous of anything that smacked of criticism of the imperial order. The church in Narcissus's household would be similarly pro-Roman and imperial but possibly less favourably disposed to Jews.

The brothers (Romans 16:14) were probably a group of low-status egalitarian self-employed workers, scratching a living at the bottom of the social pecking order. They all had slave names, which might indicate their status at the time or that of their family.

The saints were probably a group of more conservative Jewish Christians of the kind still dominant in Jerusalem. It is possible that this was the group that received the letter to the Hebrews – written a little after Romans as the clouds of Neronian persecution gathered pace in the mid-60s AD. The presence of named women in the group suggests a certain egalitarian bent, however.

Some of these groups – notably those meeting at the home of Priscilla and Aquila and in the households of Aristobulus and Narcissus – were probably composed of people of moderate means. Indeed the *apparitores* might have been comparatively quite well off. But many of the groups consisted of poorer people who would have met not in *domus*-style houses hosted by patrons but in "tenement churches", groups meeting in *insulae* or bars and cafés in Rome's poorer districts – Trastevere or Porta Capena.

Most Christians would have lived in such accommodation, so they would have had to have met as and when they could in the crowded rooms of the *insula* in which one of them lived or the workshop in which they were employed (though that would have been difficult had they not been the person renting it), or in public spaces, possibly even outside when the weather was good.

What's in a name?

Analysis of the names in Romans 16 suggests that at least a third were slaves or were descended from slaves. It is entirely likely that they had come to Rome as part of a household or had gained their freedom and migrated to the city in search of a living. What is almost certainly the case is that they would have been pretty poor people, scratching a living at the bottom of the city's food chain.

It also appears that the groups Paul refers to as the brothers (16:14) and the saints (16:15) did not have any formal leadership. This too suggests that they were from the poorer sections of the community. It is clear from the way Priscilla and Aquila are described, for instance, that they were hosts, patrons, and hence leaders of the congregation that met in their home.

But none of the five listed in Romans 16:14–15 appears to be playing the role of patron for the group. Whatever organization these groups had would have been very rudimentary indeed. Some have argued that we can see evidence for such churches in Thessalonica as well. In 2 Thessalonians 3:10 it seems that the celebration of the Lord's Supper required that everyone contribute something, as there was no patron or benefactor present who would provide from any surplus he enjoyed for those who had nothing.

Aspiring to be somebody

What emerges here is the picture of the earliest Christian communities attracting people from across the non-elite population of the city. There is no evidence until the very end of the century that anyone from the equestrian order associated themselves with this new movement. But aspiring upwardly mobile imperial administrators shared space with craft-workers and day labourers in a faith that seemed to attract people of all kinds.

When Paul wrote to the church in Corinth, he pointed out that not many of them were from the upper echelons of society (1 Corinthians

1:26–29). But it appears that there were people of varying income levels in the churches in that city, something that was causing problems within the Christian community. (See chapter 6's examination of what was happening when the churches met to share the Lord's Supper.)

This is also apparent in the fact that some in the church were able to afford to go to court (1 Corinthians 6:1–8). Access to the courts was only open to certain people in society. The poor could not afford it and those of lower social status were forbidden from taking legal action against the rich. However, it is well attested that rich people and those of the elite classes often went to court over apparently very trivial cases – for example, a man might sue a fellow dinner guest for slander because of a remark made over a meal! Paul suggests that some in the Corinthian congregations were using the courts for similarly trivial reasons.

Worship and social climbing

In 1 Corinthians 11 Paul talks about the conduct of worship and makes reference to the fact that it is undesirable for men to cover their heads when praying. Statues and other decorative artefacts show us that it was the practice of elite men – knights and senators – when leading prayer in a temple to draw their togas up over their heads. No one else did this. Paul seems to be suggesting that there were some in the Corinthian congregations who aspired to elite status and wanted everyone around them to know it.

In a long section, Paul outlines the Christian position on buying meat from the market and accepting dinner invitations (chapters 8–10). This suggests that there were in the church people rich enough to buy meat – otherwise why talk about it? – and some who were being invited to lavish banquets in temples and the homes of the wealthy where such meat would be on the menu. Such dining in the Roman world tended to be the preserve of the elite and those aspiring to join them.

It seems clear that churches were a very mixed bag. Many of those drawn to the new movement were craft-workers, some of whom made a reasonable living, while others struggled. Some worked in administration for local magistrates or even within the burgeoning imperial household and were therefore quite well off and well placed (until their eyesight began to fail and their usefulness as scribes began to diminish).

Because of this, the Christian movement was different from both the voluntary associations that were popular across the empire and the cults that people chose to join. Both of these groups tended to consist of people of one type from the same income bracket. The Christian movement was possibly the most socially mixed group in the Roman empire. That was one of its great strengths, but it was also one of the reasons why there were so many tensions that needed to be addressed in the letters sent to the groups springing up in cities across the empire by Paul and other key leaders.

In particular, the issue of how money was used to build the community life of the churches was one that both attracted converts and caused difficulties between members.

He's not heavy, he's your brother

In his first story of the earliest Christian community in Acts, Luke twice tells us that the believers had everything in common and distributed to those who were in need (Acts 2:44–45; 4:32, 34–35). This form of social organization has been described as "love communalism", a community of shared or pooled resources motivated by love between its members.

Some scholars suggest that this was a social experiment that failed. Their argument hinges on the fact that, when famine came to the region in the mid-40s AD, the Jerusalem and Judean believers did not have the resources to cope and were therefore dependent on support from elsewhere. That help arrived from Antioch in the form of the gifts from the Christians there (Acts 11:27–30; Galatians 2:1–10). Later help came from Paul, as he brought the collection that he had taken up from the predominantly Gentile churches he had planted in Jerusalem (Acts 24:17).

But such a view completely misunderstands the precarious nature of life in the first century. As noted in chapter 4 few people had the resources to be able to cope with food shortages – which usually resulted in prices of staple foods going up beyond their reach – let alone famines. The majority of Christians were middling to poor people, many living just a little above subsistence and thus vulnerable to economic downturns.

The view that the Acts experiment was soon abandoned also fails to take account of Paul's teaching that the church should function as a family. His gathering of a collection from the Gentile churches for the poor in Judea, and the mutual caring among Christians that is found in all sections of the New Testament is evidence of this.

Some historians argue that the early Christian movement was made up mainly of poor people with a few of the better off who acted as patrons and benefactors. In other words, the Christian groups operated like all other voluntary associations, with members looking to richer benefactors for support in times of need (see chapter 5).

Others argue that the early Christians practised what is called mutualism, the idea that resources are pooled – formally or informally – and distributed to those in need by those who are doing well enough at the moment on the understanding that, should they get into trouble, the same would happen for them.

This is not the same as the reciprocity we saw at work in the patronage system (see chapter 5), because that way of doing things is not fundamentally equitable. It cannot be seen as promoting the well-being of everyone involved. Patronage maintains and reinforces social divisions, but mutualism tends to break them down.

More than charity

The so-called "collection" that Paul gathered from the Gentile churches he planted to give to the Jewish believers in Jerusalem was a prime example of mutualism at work. Paul talks about it in all his major letters

(Romans 15:25-32; 1 Corinthians 16:1-4; 2 Corinthians 8-9; Galatians 2:10).

The collection had two principal aims. First, it aimed to promote material well-being – namely the relief of the acute poverty the Jerusalem churches were facing. And secondly, it was thoroughly mutual in character. It was not an act of charity. Rather it was an act of redistribution from those who had to those who did not have. And it was done in recognition of the fact that, should the positions be reversed, the present donors would be the recipients in future.

We see this clearly in 2 Corinthians 8:14, part of a long section where Paul explains the reason for the collection. Food shortages were common across the empire and this collection was a response to a local food crisis (this time in Judea). In future, cash could flow the other way if hardship hit, say, Corinth (as probably happened around the time Paul wrote 1 Corinthians) or any other part of the empire.

We see the same mutualism elsewhere in Paul's writing. For example, in 1 Thessalonians 4:9-10 "love" is seen in practical help and support offered to one another. In many ways this is the Acts 2 and 4 model in operation. That model could be seen as fundamentally mutual – people using their excess to help those with nothing with a view to ensuring no one was ever in need (including themselves should their excess ever run out and be replaced by scarcity). In 2 Thessalonians 3:6-12 it is evident that mutualism was a guiding principle of economic relations both between and within the early Christian communities.

Such mutualism undermines the ideas of benefaction and patronage that we have seen to be at the heart of how Romans saw society working. Paul urges everyone to become a benefactor in the sense of doing good in their community without the expectation of getting anything in return. Paul himself offered a model of hard work and paying his own way to the new believers in Thessalonica, something he reminds them of in 1 Thessalonians 2:1-10 and 2 Thessalonians 3:6-12.

Because the Christian communities were economically mixed, there were wealthier householders who acted as patrons to a number of clients. For example, Acts tells us about a man called Aristarchus (19:29 and

20:4). He might well have been one of the *politarchs* of the city and hence a man of some means. Jason, in whose workshop, it seems, Paul made tents and gossiped the gospel, was not on the breadline. And Acts 17:4 suggests some wealthier women were attracted to the movement.

Don't patronize me

The presence in the church of people who would inevitably have been patrons and benefactors by dint of their wealth and social position posed a bit of a problem for Paul. He was keen for everyone in the church to work so as to have something to share with those in need and, more importantly, so as not to be dependent on anybody else.

There were food shortages in Thessalonica, across the whole of Macedonia and, in the early 50s, Corinth – after Paul had planted the church but possibly before he wrote to them. There was some public welfare available to some of Thessalonica's Roman citizens in the form of the grain dole (see chapter 4). Wealthy people could afford to buy food at whatever inflated prices were being charged. Slaves and freedmen would receive food from their masters or former masters.

But what of the poor and those who worked with their hands? Historians suggest that they shared as best they could but that many would have starved at such times. Such people would jump at the chance of receiving food from a wealthy patron. Paul urges the Christians to share what they have with those in need but not on the basis of the patronage system but rather out of mutual regard for one another.

And what did Paul want to see happen as the shortages eased? Did these poor Christians remain in client–patron relationships with wealthier benefactors? It seems that they did and this is why Paul wrote such strong words to those who chose not to work but to live as clients of wealthy benefactors.

His aim was nothing less than the abolition of the patronage system through the practice of mutualism that had at its heart individuals working with their hands when they were able to, so they would have

Is He One of Us?

One of the things that makes it difficult to assess what was really happening in the Roman economy is the attitude of the contemporary authors. They tended to write about Roman society in terms of stark contrasts.

They tended to see society made up of just two groups: the honestiores – the honourable, rich elite minority – and the humiliores – basically the great unwashed rest. As far as these witnesses were concerned people were either part of the elite, and therefore were rich and cultured, or they were not, and so were simply "the poor".

Occasionally authors distinguished between the deserving poor and the dirty plebs. The former were usually associated with the great houses and families as either favourite slaves or freedmen. The latter were simply the undifferentiated mass of the population, which these writers tried to avoid at all costs!

But even these authors realized that this was not a description of reality but a piece of rhetoric that enabled them to justify why the ruling elite enjoyed the position they did in society. Their writings served to reinforce the strict social hierarchy and keep the poor in their place.

The second-century author Aelius Aristides spells it out: "The existence of inferiors is an advantage to superiors since they will be able to point out those over whom they are superior." So they were uninterested in investigating their world to see if there were gradations of poverty, if some workers were living better than others. They were only interested in ensuring that the current social order carried on undisturbed. It is why some at the end of the first and beginning of the second century began to see the Christian movement as a threat to that order.

something to share with those who had fallen on hard times and would in turn receive support if hard times came their way.

His emphasis on economic self-sufficiency meant that Christians were able to live lives of generosity, giving without any expectation of being repaid. In this he echoes Jesus in the Sermon on the Mount. Paul longed to see the creation of communities where there was no one in need and where this desire to do good spilled out into the world around the church. No wonder the Christian message was so attractive to poor and middling sorts, whose lives could be very precarious.

Do some good

Paul urged all Christians to give to meet real needs (Paul appealed to Titus to ensure that the Christians on Crete behaved in such a way in Titus 3:14) – but not patrons. The difference in Paul's eyes was that a Christian benefactor gave because he or she could, whereas a patron gave to further his or her own ambitions in society.

Paul's ethic of doing good to all grew out of his understanding of the church as a family (see chapter 6), a place where all the members were equal regardless of their social status or economic position.

CHAPTER 8

A SUPERMARKET OF FAITHS

Everywhere you went in Roman cities you fell over gods. Shrines stood on street corners, temples dominated the skylines of city centres, household gods stood on shelves and in cubby holes in homes and shops, and rituals gave shape to most people's days.

The empire swarmed with religions, philosophies, and beliefs of every conceivable type. Judea might have stood out in this world because it was firmly monotheistic, but even Galilee where Jesus had grown up had more than its fair share of pagan temples and shrines, a legacy of generations of Greco-Roman influence. The cities of Sepphoris and Tiberias could have been places where the carpenter Jesus plied his trade with other craft-workers, building a whole range of grand structures, including temples to a variety of Greek and Roman gods.

The early Christians proclaimed their message of the coming kingdom of Israel's one God to people not lacking religious options.

Join our gang

As the Roman empire spread across the lands that had once been the heart of Alexander the Great's Greek empire, so their gods mingled with the gods of the Greeks. There was a particular identification between the key Roman deities – Jupiter, Juno, Minerva, Venus, Diana, Mercury, Mars, Pluto, Neptune, Bacchus – and the Greek pantheon – Zeus, Hera, Athena, Aphrodite, Artemis, Hermes, Ares, Hades, Poseidon, Dionysus, Apollo. But Greek and Roman styles of worship were different. So religion in the west of the empire differed from that in the more Hellenistic east. But eastern cults became increasingly popular in Rome, Ostia, and Pompeii. In particular, there is abundant evidence of the popularity of the Egyptian cult of Isis, as well as the Asian cult of Cybele, at the heart of the empire.

The Romans had a particularly unique way of acquiring gods. When they laid siege to a city or were crossing the borders of a new land, they held a ceremony called the *evocatio*. Priests would formally acknowledge the gods of the enemy city and then invite them to abandon it and join the Roman pantheon. And so the choice of gods was swelled every time Rome added a new territory.

The Greek world was a collection of independent city-states, each with its own deity, or individual take on a deity from the pantheon. The cities had many temples and everyone participated in the public ceremonies that ensured the gods would look favourably on them.

In Thessalonica, for example, one of the key cults centred on a deity called Cabirus, whose image was on the coinage and whose festivals dominated the religious calendar. He was a deified hero from Thessalonica's distant past, an ordinary, even poor, working man who had died defending the city from its enemies. The myth had grown up that, in times of peril, he would return to defend the city again, especially the hard-working poor.

The symbol of the cult was a hammer because it was particularly associated with the craft-workers of the city. But the fact that city coins bore his image and everyone joined in festivals in his honour meant that worship of Cabirus was significant to the city as a whole. And it is possible that Paul's message about a working man crucified by his enemies but raised to life and returning to rescue his own from the present evil age would have gained a ready hearing among the working people of Thessalonica – this is certainly the impression we get from the book of Acts and Paul's letters to the church in the city.

Making sense of the world

The Roman world sought peace with the gods – the *pax decorum* (a sort of spiritual equivalent of the *pax Romana* that held the empire together). All disasters that befell the empire were blamed on that *pax* being breached by human disrespect for the divine order – and especially by irregular or new forms of worship. Public ceremonies, during which sacrifices were made and prayers offered, were important occasions in which all citizens were expected to participate.

Right across the empire, these ceremonies were formal civic affairs. To participate in them, you did not have to believe that the deity was particularly interested in your town, or to have the deity as part of your household's collection of gods. The cult rather tended to function as the glue that held a city or community together.

But this did not mean that the ceremonies were taken lightly. Statues and stone reliefs from all over the empire show how central these rituals were to civic life. So although Roman religion did not have a central creed binding believers together, or a book – like the Bible – containing laws and stories shared by everyone, there was a set of rituals and actions that everyone knew had to happen for the gods to be supportive of human endeavours.

Roman religion was not really a way of life, either. There was no moral code at the heart of worship that was backed by the gods and marked the sort of behaviour expected by those gods of their adherents to distinguish them from others. But there was an understanding that, if the rituals were properly followed, then the gods would ensure the continued security of the city.

This was reinforced by the notions of *pietas* and *impietas*. *Pietas* was marked by doing one's duty by one's family and others in the community and observing the norms of behaviour expected in society. *Impietas* was its opposite. But these were less religious concepts than general notions of doing the right thing to preserve the social order.

So Octavian was commended for acting in accordance with *pietas* in raising an army to avenge the death of his adopted father Julius Caesar. Following the establishment of the imperial government under Octavian (renamed Augustus following his victory) *impietas*, understood as thinking and acting in ways that unsettled the relationships between Caesar, the people, and the gods, became one of the definitions of treason. To behave badly toward the government was by definition to offend the gods who supported that government. There was no separation of church and state in the ancient world.

So Roman religion was less a matter of private belief than it was of public behaviour and in particular of participation in public rituals.

Winning divine favour

The central ritual was animal sacrifice, something that happened on a podium at the top of the steps leading into a temple rather than in the temple itself, because worship was a formal public act, to be witnessed by as many people as possible. Indeed the interiors of temples tended to be storehouses for valuables rather than places where congregations gathered to worship.

Such rituals were not carried out by religious professionals but by members of the city's ruling elite – thus showing the close link between human authority and the power of the gods. A stone relief from Pompeii shows a member of the town's magistracy, with his toga drawn up over his head as was the rule when officiating at a sacrifice, saying prayers and offering wine and incense. Meanwhile three figures, stripped to the waist, probably slaves of the elite man conducting the ceremony, are leading a bull toward the altar. One of them carries the axe that will be used to slaughter the animal. It is those three that will be covered in blood and gore as the sacrifice is made, not the gentleman officiating.

Once slaughtered, parts of the animal would be burned on the altar to please the god in whose honour the sacrifice was being made and the rest of the animal would be butchered and the meat offered to worshippers, possibly as a gift or possibly through the meat market, which was handily situated very near the complex where most of the temples were. That all depended on the reason for the sacrifice and the festival being celebrated.

It is probably not true to say that most meat sold through the markets had first been sacrificed in temples but a good amount of it had and it is clear that this caused the early Christians a good deal of difficulty (see, in particular, Paul's discussion of the problem of meat offered to idols in 1 Corinthians 8–10).

Fun for all the family

These religious rituals were at the heart of the community's life. Special festivals were often accompanied by games and dramas performed on the steps of the temples. There was often feasting for everyone – including the poor, who would receive a meagre portion of the sacrificed beast and wine to wash it down.

Such sacrifices reminded everyone of their place in the world. On a large canvas it pictured human beings standing midway between the gods and the animals offered on the altars. Within the city, it reminded everyone of their place in the social pecking order.

Everyone was expected to attend and join in. And why wouldn't you? Major festivals meant a day off work for most (many slaves were needed to serve on these occasions) and there was free food and entertainment. For a few days of the year, the whole community came together to celebrate the goodness of the gods and the social order over which they presided. Not to join in was to invite suspicion. And the followers of Jesus found it impossible to join in. They rejected the sacrifices at the heart of Roman religion, believing that the one sacrifice for the good of all people had been made through the cross of Christ and that all others were idolatry. Such behaviour looked like atheism, the charge that many Christians faced in the second century, something that would have baffled and appalled their neighbours.

A message in the offal?

The internal organs of the animal being sacrificed, especially the liver, would be used to discern the disposition of the gods – were they looking favourably on the city or not? Such discernment was in the hands of a skilled reader of livers, known as the *haruspex*. Most cities had such a person in the highest echelons of government; the emperor always had one on his staff.

Few important decisions were made without consulting the *haruspex* or some other augur who was on hand to predict whether an enterprise being considered would meet with success or not. The augurs used a variety of means to receive messages from the gods. Livers were examined, birds were watched, unusual events were monitored and interpreted, and pages of the Sibylline oracles were read at random.

There were many stories told to warn people of the danger that was risked in ignoring the advice of the augurs. One such concerned a consul of Rome, Appius Claudius Pulcher, commander of Rome's fleet in 249 BC, who went into battle against the Carthaginians despite the auguries being against it. On board his flagship sacred chickens were used to predict whether the gods favoured a course of action or not. The idea was that if the chickens ate, the auspices were good; if they ate so greedily that bits of food were falling from their beaks, the auspices were excellent. But if the birds abstained from eating altogether, it was best to go home and do nothing.

Appius Claudius Pulcher was determined to go into battle. The chickens were consulted. They resolutely refused so much as to peck at a grain. The furious consul pitched them overboard, saying: "If they won't eat, let them drink." They drowned and he sailed to total defeat. The chickens were not to be trifled with: this was the message that everyone heard as that story was told and retold!

The state of worship

The fastest growing religion in the first century was the imperial cult. It had begun when the Roman senate declared that Julius Caesar had become a god on his death and by implication his adopted son Augustus was also therefore divine. People began to offer incense and prayers *to* the emperor and not just *for* him and his family, especially in the east of the empire where worship of great leaders of the past was an established practice.

To begin with the imperial cult honoured dead Caesars, but fairly early on, living ones saw the benefit of being treated like gods and so gave permission for shrines and even temples to be built in their honour. So in Pergamum, in modern-day Turkey, a temple to Augustus was consecrated in 27 BC, the year he became Caesar. By the time of Domitian in the AD 80s, the cult appears to have become central to civic life across the empire. And certainly by the time of Pliny, in the early second century, failure to burn incense to Caesar's image was enough to get a Christian – or anyone else, but only Christians found such an act impossible – condemned to death.

The imperial cult termed Caesar both *soter* (saviour) and *kurios* (Lord), terms used by the Christians from as early as the AD 30s. From Augustus onwards, Caesar was also known as "son of god" because Augustus was the adopted son of the deified Julius Caesar. The poet Virgil in the epic poem *The Aeneid* said of him: "This is he whom you have so often heard promised to you, Augustus Caesar, son of a god, who shall again set up the golden age." He and many in Rome believed that Augustus's victory in the civil war that followed the death of Julius Caesar was evidence of the new Caesar's divinity.

An inscription found in the Greek city of Priene probably dating from the early first century AD suggests that Augustus's birthday would become New Year's Day and that there would be feasting and celebrations on that day because of its significance. It reads:

Since Providence, which has ordered all things and is deeply interested in our life, has set in most perfect order by giving us Augustus, whom she filled with virtue that he might benefit humankind, sending him as a saviour, both for us and for our descendants, that he might end war and arrange all things, and since he, Caesar, by his appearance (excelling even our anticipations), surpassed all previous benefactors, and did not even leave to posterity any hope of surpassing what he has done, and since the birthday of the god Augustus was the beginning of the good tidings for the world that came by reason of him.

A god in every home

Religion was not just a matter of civic ceremony. Just about every home had a *lar*, a household god, who was set on a *lararium*, a shelf or open cupboard that served as a shrine in the house. Every morning the head of the house would offer something to the household god in the hope of his or her protection over the family through that day. The offering would most likely be a little food or incense burned in a censer before the tiny statue of the deity.

In some homes, the *lararium* was painted on the wall in one of the rooms or at the back of the peristyle. Those who lived in *insulae* might have a simple shelf with one or more rough wooden or stone statuettes of a *lar* to whom they looked for good fortune.

From Pompeii and other places we know that workplaces also contained *lararia*, the god of the trade or traders set to watch over the working day. The presence of such statues served to reassure customers and clients coming into the shop that the traders were pious and thus trustworthy.

There was a problem for early followers of Jesus who may well have removed their household gods from their previous prominent places in home and workshop. This could lead to accusations of *impietas*, dishonouring the gods, disrupting the social fabric in a way that might affect everyone. The upshot of this could have been loss of trade and income for a Christian family, investigation of their activities by the local magistrate, even violence against them perpetrated by suspicious and fearful neighbours.

Finding gods at the crossroads

Beyond the home and workshop, temple and *popina*, gods were honoured at roadside shrines, especially at important junctions and crossroads. In Rome and other cities, local officials (*vicomagistri* in Rome) put up altars and shrines to gods at crossroads, ensured that the suitable rituals took place at them each day, and oversaw their general maintenance and upkeep.

The officials responsible tended not to be leading citizens, but ordinary people who lived nearby and earned a small salary combining

A Curse on You

One of the features of Roman religion was its offer to get a god to do something for you. There were rituals that were designed to yield a favourable response to requests for success in business or in love.

Graffiti from Pompeii's theatre asks Venus to look kindly on two lovers. And in the house of Julius Polybius graffiti written by a slave seeks the safe return of the master and is accompanied by a vow made to the household god, suggesting that, as well as writing, the slave was making an offering of incense or food. But the gods were also invoked in disputes. And this could well be the context for some puzzling words that we find in 1 Corinthians 12:2–3. There the apostle says that no one speaking by God's Spirit says "Jesus curse". Most translations (including the New RSV) add the verb "be" in order to try to make sense of Paul's words. But this is unnecessary when seen against a back-drop of Roman religion.

In Corinth and a host of other places hundreds of so-called curse tablets have been found. These were written by a priest or sorcerer on behalf of the worshipper and then dropped down a well or left at a shrine. The tablets contain pretty simple messages such as "Maxima Pontia, for destruction" or "Drucus, fail in business".

The idea of these was very simple. The devotee invoked a god – usually one of the deities associated with the underworld, such as Pluto – to curse the named person. Part of Roman religion was about getting the gods to do one's bidding by performing the correct ritual and observing the sacrifices. It was based on the social idea of reciprocity (see Chapter 5).

It appears from what Paul writes to the church in Corinth that some Christians were carrying these practices over into their life as followers of Jesus. And just as they had invoked the gods they previously followed to bring blessings to them and curses on their enemies, so they expected Jesus to act in the same way.

This, of course, was the absolute antithesis of what Jesus stood for. He had taught that we love our enemies and Paul instructed his congregations not to repay curses for curses but to overcome evil with good (Romans 12:14, 17–21).

So here, in 1 Corinthians 12:2–3, Paul is saying that no one who is inspired by the Spirit of God can use Jesus to invoke a curse on an opponent – a business rival or someone with whom they are in a legal dispute or, even worse, another church member with whom they have a disagreement.

this role with civic duties such as watching for fires, trying to keep the traffic moving in the chaos of the streets, and keeping an eye open for crime. Here civic and religious duties were seamlessly bound together, showing that religion was not a separate, private practice in Roman cities.

The *vicomagistri* and other officials charged with this duty were invariably men. Women did not do very well when religious roles were being handed out in Roman society. Most officiating priests at shrines and temples were elite males assisted by male slaves or freedmen – though women sometimes played a supporting role.

The only significant place in traditional Roman religion for women outside the home was through becoming a vestal virgin – and this was only open to a very few women, perhaps six at any one time. These public priestesses served for thirty years, having been given to the order when they were between six and ten years old. One of their key roles was to guard the sacred flame that constantly burned in the temple of Vesta by Rome's forum. If they failed to remain chaste through their term of office, they were buried alive within the confines of the temple.

Wives of the elite men who served as priests sometimes had a role alongside their husbands at formal ceremonies. Otherwise, women were only allowed prominent roles in religious activities that were exclusively female. Venus cults, for example, were popular in many cities, where elite and non-elite women gathered to honour the goddess through rituals and good works. They were often a means for the ruling classes to promote and impose elite values on women whose behaviour was morally questionable and certainly violated the more conservative laws that had been passed by Augustus to bolster family life in the empire.

But generally women were participants but not leaders in Roman religion. Those seeking more of a role needed to look to one of the cults that arose at the eastern end of the empire and became popular through early imperial times, cults such as those of Isis, Cybele, and Dionysus. Here women could play much greater roles in leadership.

Pick a god

Those looking for a more intimate religious experience turned to the plethora of mystery cults. These were often associated with particular places or trades or social classes or cohorts in the legion. Devotees who chose to join these cults underwent initiation rituals – often involving a "baptism" of some kind – and took part in regular offering of sacrifices and prayers in order to ensure that the cult god would look favourably on them.

The mystery cults gave their adherents a sense of belonging often absent from the more formal religious activities. They also promised access to divine power and immortality. They offered a personal rather than civic salvation. And they often gave women a significant role in leadership to which they could not aspire in traditional Roman worship. So they were very popular.

But they struggled to gain acceptance in the west. The cults of Isis, Cybele, and Dionysus were marked by ecstatic worship, often featuring particularly frenzied processions and festivals. So, although it had been present in Rome since the third century BC, it was only in AD 50 that Claudius allowed members of the Roman elite of either sex to become priests in the Cybele cult in Rome.

The cult of Isis originated in Egypt but became the fastest growing cult in the empire apart from the worship of Caesar. Its growth in the first and second centuries certainly outstripped that of the Christian faith, which for the first 200 years of its life was relatively small and so insignificant as to be all but invisible in many places.

This cult was a religion with drama, blood, and guts, full of revenge and table-turning, which seemed to touch something deep in the Roman psyche. It was an exotic cult, full of mystery and the glamour of Egypt. In fact, one of the reasons why it did not come completely to dominate the religious scene as the empire matured was that it never lost its Egyptian identity. It resisted attempts by Roman writers to help it accommodate to Roman ways of thinking. Its priesthood in Egypt refused to allow its core texts to be translated from the hieroglyphs in which they were written. So, in more ways than one, it remained a mystery.

But that was part of its appeal. It was no formal, impersonal religion: it was a vibrant, visceral, emotional, and above all personal faith that promised encounter with the god at its heart through its rituals and ceremonies.

Everyone loves a mystery

At the heart of the cult of Isis was a powerful story. Her husband Osiris was killed and dismembered by his nephew Seth. Isis put the body together again and breathed fresh life into it; their child, Horus, exacted revenge on Seth for what he had done.

Here was religion as soap opera, as family saga. But in particular, here was religion that offered the promise of life after death – something traditional Roman religion was a bit vague about – and a central, starring role for a female deity. It was not that Rome had no female gods – Venus and Diana are prime examples – but there was something about Isis that offered Roman women hope.

And they took it. Evidence from Pompeii, Ostia, Rome, and other cities suggests that the cult of Isis attracted large numbers of women from all levels of society. The temple in Pompeii happens to be among the best preserved of the town's buildings. It was small, surrounded by a well laid out and lavishly decorated courtyard. It was surrounded by a high wall, making it a discreet, almost private place. The cult was for the initiated, not all and sundry – and that was part of its appeal. You had to choose to get involved. And a steep learning curve was involved if you did. The Egyptian paintings on the wall of one of the rooms of the temple complex indicate that there was a lot of information to take on board as you joined the cult.

Male members only

While Isis and Cybele appealed to women, the cult of Mithras was for men only. Mithraism probably originated in Persia but it spread quickly west, gaining popularity especially among soldiers and army veterans because of its emphasis on discipline and hierarchy. It really took off in the second century AD but was already popular in the first.

Like Isis, the cult of Mithras was for the initiated only. Its temples tended to be in basements with ante-rooms preventing the curious from entering the main sanctuary where the altar was situated. Very little is known for certain about how the cult operated and what devotees believed. Sculptures tell us that Mithras was born from rock and sacrificed a bull, possibly the divine bull of Persian mythology from whose blood all living beings were created.

The fact that the archaeological evidence for the cult appears quite suddenly and in a variety of places has suggested to some historians that the cult was in fact a Roman invention, closely linked to the army. It certainly offered a robust religious experience to men. It also seems to have had close links with astrology, which appealed to a fatalistic trait in the Roman approach to life. From the temple remains, it is also clear that feasting was a central part of Mithraic practice – something else that would have appealed to Roman men.

The battle for ideas

Many found what was on offer in terms of religious practice absolutely to their taste. But others did not. There is evidence that by the first century there was a growing disenchantment with religion of all kinds. People were still joining in with the festivals and rituals; they were just not finding them altogether satisfying. This led to renewed interest in philosophy and ideas.

It needs to be stressed that most philosophers of this age were not atheists, and people meeting to talk about the latest theories might go on from there to worship in a public temple or private mystery cult. But there certainly was an interest in other ways of seeing the world from those offered by the religious hierarchies.

The Epicureans, for instance, though believing in the gods, thought religion irrelevant to life. They believed everything could be explained

Epictetus

The world of the early church was a world full of philosophers. Across the empire, stoics, Epicureans, cynics, and others vied for attention in a market-place of ideas. And their words – often heard as philosophers lectured in the market-squares – formed the background noise in which the new teaching about Jesus was being heard.

Epictetus was a stoic philosopher who lived from around AD 55 to 135. He was born a slave in Hierapolis in modern-day Turkey, lived in Rome for a time, and ended his days as a teacher in Nicopolis in Greece. Interestingly, Paul wrote to Titus from this city some thirty years before Epictetus took up residence, indicating the presence of a church on the philosopher's doorstep.

His teaching has come down to us because of the diligence of his student Flavius Arrian (c. 86–160), an elite Roman who would serve in public office under Hadrian. He wrote verbatim accounts of Epictetus's lectures that he collected in two works: the *Discourses* and the *Handbook*.

In his lifetime Epictetus was a popular and sought-after teacher, with students coming from all over the empire to study under him. The reason for this is probably because he was a plain-speaking man who was only really interested in telling people how the good life could be found. The popularity of his teaching – and no doubt that of countless others like him – suggests a hunger in the empire for down-to-earth lifestyle advice.

Epictetus was interested in the outcome or effect of what people believed. He taught the very Socratic idea that a student must know himself and live out of a firm moral purpose. For this reason he was not impressed by the revival of the sophist movement occurring in Greece, especially in Corinth, with its emphasis on splendid rhetoric and star billing for the philosopher himself.

A sophist who visited his school boasted of the way he took care of his appearance, set his hair, and wore jewellery so that his audience would think well of him even before he opened his mouth. He told Epictetus that the people "like smooth men".

Epictetus was much more interested in inner beauty. It was living according to the cardinal virtues – piety, justice, and self-control. This was a matter of substance, not style. As his old teacher, the Roman stoic Musonius Rufus, had said: "If you have nothing better to do than to praise me, then I am speaking to no purpose." The point of any discourse was that it would inform how to live.

And the reason for coming to a philosopher was not only to hear how to live but to see it as well. A philosopher's pupils were urged to imitate their teacher's way of thinking and living. In this way they would achieve happiness, the goal of all good teaching.

Epictetus seems to have been aware of the presence of the church in his city because he twice makes reference to "the Galileans" in the *Discourses*. But what he has to say does not suggest that he took much notice; this was just another sect among the many that vied for people's attention in the urban landscape.

through the interaction of natural forces and believed strongly in free will, in contrast to most citizens who were very fatalistic, feeling their lives were in the grip of forces beyond their control. The purpose of Epicurean ideas was to free people from superstition and fear. Life was for living and to be enjoyed, and hence they got a bit of a reputation for being profligate and decadent.

The stoics, on the other hand, sought to live lives of reverence, believing all things to be god. Their key concern was how we might live an ethical life in harmony with the natural order; and that differed from person to person. So stoicism was a fiercely individualistic creed and one characterized by asceticism. Unlike Epicureanism, stoicism was not a school for parties.

The cynics, who predated and gave rise to the stoics, also believed that life should be lived according to nature. For the cynics this meant lives of the utmost simplicity. Their founder, Diogenes, lived in a barrel, with only a cloak and cup to his name – eventually he even gave up the cup. Cynics rejected social norms and lived as wandering beggars, uttering aphorisms that many regarded as wise and others as nonsense.

Other schools also blossomed and in many cities – as Paul discovered in Athens – there were lively debating groups eager to discuss the latest ideas and find the key to the good life everyone wanted. It should be stressed, however, that the Areopagus, before which Paul appeared in

Athens, was not a debating society but the legislative body that regulated the establishment of new ideas and religions in the city. Paul was really on trial before it.

In Corinth, people prized good philosophy and good arguments delivered in crisp and flowing rhetoric. It was something of a centre for ideas, frequently visited by the leading thinkers in various schools of philosophy throughout the first century. And part of the problem that Paul encountered in the church here was that it seemed to be more interested in style than substance, in the rhetoric the message was couched in rather than the message itself.

The attractions of Christianity

The new message about Jesus that came to Roman cities from the eastern end of the empire struck various chords with its first audience.

Like the mystery cults, it offered personal encounter with a god. But unlike those cults, the God at the heart of the Christian message was full of love and sympathy for weak humanity. His was not a message of graft but of grace. He was not inviting initiates on an endless treadmill of rituals but to a life of freedom based on a single one-time only sacrifice of Jesus, the Son of God.

In particular, it seemed to appeal to ordinary working people because the central figure of the faith was himself a working man, a carpenter. But, more than that, the people who brought the faith to the cities of the empire were also working people – fishermen such as Peter, tent-makers such as Paul, Aquila and Priscilla, traders such as Lydia and Phoebe. This was not a faith of the elite designed to confirm the current social order. Rather it was a message that suggested all people were equal and that social hierarchies were not part of God's grand plan.

So the faith caught on in the back streets of the empire's cities. It was never a mass movement in the early days. The gatherings of the early churches in the houses and apartments of those first followers were small and intimate. But it established a significant foothold so that, when the going got really tough for Christians in the early second century, the faith was sufficiently robust and established to withstand the pressure.

By the turn of the third century, when the cults of Isis and Mithras were at their peak, the cult of Jesus of Nazareth was gaining a reputation for morality and good behaviour that surpassed anything other cults could generate. A concern not just for their own but for their neighbours, even when it got them into trouble with the authorities, did not go unnoticed.

The centre of Christian worship

What distinguished the Christian movement from almost every other religious activity in the empire was that it had no temple and made no sacrifices. Even the Jewish people, until AD 70 when it was destroyed by the Roman armies, had a temple with a calendar dominated by festivals involving sacrifices.

We saw in earlier chapters that the basic Christian gathering happened at a meal in the ordinary homes of the members and that this was the case for at least the first 200 years of the movement (see chapters 4 and 5).

They met to eat in order to remember the sacrifice that created their movement in the first place – that of Jesus on the cross. No one in these gatherings was required to fulfil the roles that priests had in the Roman cults. And because the Christians did not practise divination using animal behaviour or entrails but rather spoke God's words to one another, it meant that everyone who gathered was equally able to join in the symposium-style meeting at the heart of the movement (see 1 Corinthians 14:1–20).

So, if there was no sacrifice or divination – the two key features of Roman religions – what was at the heart of Christian gatherings? Jesus. The early church met in his name to remember his sacrifice and to learn his way of living by hearing and talking about his teaching. The churches met to discover what his coming into the world meant for the world and for their lives within it.

And this is why there are collections of stories about Jesus' life. These stories circulated orally for some years before being written down in the four collections we know as gospels. They were taken from place to place by the travelling Christians – such as Paul, Priscilla and Aquila, Lydia, Phoebe, Peter, and a host of unnamed missionaries – who told the story of who Jesus was and what he had done, and gathered together groups of people who wanted to know more and live his way of life. These groups were called churches (as we saw earlier the Greek word *ekklesia* seems to have been chosen precisely because it was a general word for a gathering and not a religious word at all).

He turned out to be God

The amazing thing about the person at the heart of the Christian faith was that, from very early on, the churches believed that he was in fact God in a human body. Unlike some of the gods worshipped elsewhere in the empire, who had started as mere mortals – such as Cabirus in Thessalonica and Caesar in Rome – and who had been pronounced divine after their deaths, Jesus was seen to have been God all along, who for thirty years or so became human. Much later in the development of Christian teaching, this view would be called the doctrine of the incarnation.

But for the early believers, as they told and retold the stories about Jesus and as they experienced his risen life in their midst through the presence and power of the Holy Spirit, they came to believe that this carpenter from Nazareth was God and had always been God, and that by some mystery he had become a man to share our humanity, with its struggles and uncertainties, to die for our sins, and to rise from death to offer a new way of living in the world that would go on forever.

So they naturally started calling Jesus "saviour" and "Lord" and "Son of God" and "king of kings" and the one who brings the new age of God's kingdom into the world. They found this language in what we now call the Old Testament, the scriptures of the Hebrew people, which was the only Bible the early Christians had. They found the language in the life of King

David, in the worship of the Psalms and the dreams of the prophets. But they also heard the language in the streets of the cities where they lived.

Who calls the shots?

This language was also used of Caesar. It is found on stone inscriptions in temples and market-squares that tell the story of Augustus's rise, of his triumph in the civil wars and his bringing of peace, the *pax Romana*, to the whole world. This was Caesar's gospel (they even used the Greek word *euangelion*, which means "gospel", to describe this story: the very word the Christians chose for their story). So when the believers in Corinth and Rome, Ephesus and Antioch, Jerusalem and Pergamum declared that Jesus was Lord, they were making a political statement as well as a religious one. Just as when the citizens in those same cities gathered to honour Caesar at the feast of his birthday and cried "Caesar is Lord" before his shrine as incense was burned and offerings made, they were making a religious statement as well as a political one.

When Paul wrote to the churches in the Roman colony of Philippi in the mid-50s AD that Jesus was Lord, that he had been given the name above all names, and that at his name everyone should bow and declare him Lord (Philippians 2:9–11), how would their neighbours have heard those words?

The basic Christian confession was simply this: that Israel's God had kept his promise to redeem the world through a descendant of Abraham, to send a king who would bring justice and equity, peace and wholeness to the whole of creation; and he had kept that promise in Jesus of Nazareth, crucified and raised, now Lord and saviour of all. It was an amazing claim to be heard on the lips of the devotees of a tiny cult from an obscure backwater of the empire. But it was one they believed passionately and wherever they made it, people around said they were "turning the world upside down" (Acts 17:6–7).

NOW READ THESE . . .

I hope this has whetted your appetite to delve further into the history of the early church and find out more about the early Christians and how what they believed marked them out from their neighbours.

So here are some introductory and intermediate-level books to help you on your way.

Outlines of life in the Roman empire

Gregory S. Aldrete, *Daily Life in the Roman City* (Norman: University of Oklahoma Press, 2004).

Mary Beard, *Pompeii: The Life of a Roman Town* (London: Profile Books, 2009).

John R. Clarke, *Art in the Lives of Ordinary Romans* (Berkeley: University of California Press, 2003).

Peter Garnsey and Richard Saller, *The Roman Empire: Economy, Society and Culture* (Berkeley: University of California Press, 2005).

Martin Goodman, *The Roman World 44 BC – AD 180* (Abingdon: Routledge, 1997).

James Jeffers, *The Greco-Roman World of the New Testament Era* (Downers Grove: IVP, 1999).

D. S. Potter and D. J. Mattingly, *Life, Death and Entertainment in the Roman Empire* (University of Michigan Press, 1999).

Rodney Stark, *The Rise of Christianity* (San Francisco: HarperCollins, 1997).

Andrew Wallace-Hadrill, *Houses and Society in Pompeii and Herculaneum* (Princeton: Princeton University Press, 1994).

Colin Wells, *The Roman Empire* (London: Fontana, second edition, 1992).

Paul Zanker, *Pompeii: Public and Private Life* (Cambridge, Mass.: Harvard University Press, 1998).

Accounts of the early Christians

Richard S. Ascough, *Lydia: Paul's Cosmopolitan Hostess* (Collegeville, Minn.: Michael Glazer, 2009).

Gary Burge, Lynn Cohick, and Gene Green, *The New Testament in Antiquity* (Grand Rapids: Zondervan, 2009).

David A. deSilva, *Honour, Patronage, Kinship & Purity* (Downers Grove: IVP, 2000).

Bruce W. Longenecker, *The Lost Letters of Pergamum* (Grand Rapids: Baker, 2005).

Wayne A. Meeks, *The First Urban Christians* (New Haven: Yale, 1983).

Peter Oakes, *Reading Romans in Pompeii* (London/Minneapolis: SPCK/Fortress, 2009).

Carolyn Osiek and David Balch, *Families in the New Testament World* (Louisville: Westminster, 1997).

David M. Scholer, *Social Distinctives of the Christians in the First Century: Pivotal Essays by E. A. Judge* (Peabody, Mass.: Hendrickson, 2008).

John Stambaugh and David Balch, *The Social World of the First Christians* (London: SPCK, 1986).

Todd Still and David Horrell, *After the First Urban Christians* (London: T & T Clark, 2010).

Bruce W. Winter, *After Paul Left Corinth* (Grand Rapids/ Cambridge: Eerdmans, 2001).

Penguin Classics publish accessible editions of works by all the Roman writers referred to in the text.

INDEX

Lightning Source UK Ltd.
Milton Keynes UK
UKHW010630061118
331828UK00007B/376/P